Hillsville Remembered

TRAVIS A. ROUNTREE

HILLSVILLE REMEMBERED

PUBLIC MEMORY, HISTORICAL SILENCE, *AND* APPALACHIA'S MOST NOTORIOUS SHOOT-OUT

Scholarly publisher for the Commonwealth,
serving Bellarmine University, Berea College, Centre
College of Kentucky, Eastern Kentucky University,
The Filson Historical Society, Georgetown College,
Kentucky Historical Society, Kentucky State University,
Morehead State University, Murray State University,
Northern Kentucky University, Spalding University,
Transylvania University, University of Kentucky,
University of Louisville, University of Pikeville,
and Western Kentucky University.

Editorial and Sales Offices: The University Press of Kentucky
663 South Limestone Street, Lexington, Kentucky 40508-4008
www.kentuckypress.com

Cataloging-in-Publication data is available from the Library of Congress.

ISBN 978-0-8131-9722-7 (hardcover)
ISBN 978-0-8131-9723-4 (pdf)
ISBN 978-0-8131-9724-1 (epub)

This book is printed on acid-free paper meeting the requirements of the American National Standard for Permanence in Paper for Printed Library Materials.

Manufactured in the United States of America

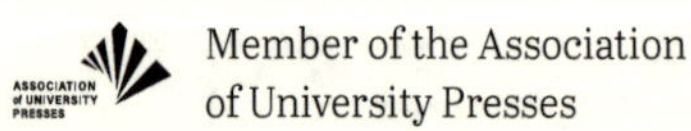

This book is dedicated to my grandparents:
Bernard Kenneth Allen
Helen Marion Allen
James Berry Rountree
Gladys Horne Rountree
Memory and story is where this book started and how each of you will live forever.

Contents

Introduction

> What did happen here there have been so many tales and outright lies told. It has been hard to see through the smoke to see the truth. Now memory, memory is like a loaded pistol it can turn again who's a-holdin' it.
>
> J. Sidna Allen in *Thunder in the Hills*
> by Frank Levering[1]

"Are you an Allen?"

He stood there hearing what the man said. The question brought thoughts into his mind.

Was he an Allen?

The oldest of five, he remembered his own father. "Orphaned" is what the state had written on the birth certificate. His father—a tall, powerful presence—was known to come to violence quickly. He was a moonshiner in Powhatan County, Virginia. He had a scar on his face that reflected a time when he jumped a fence to escape federal agents and got his face caught on the barbwire, only for a second, before sprinting away in the darkness, bleeding. Violence begets violence, but was his own daddy tied to this place? Could his daddy have been an orphan from the shoot-out that happened here in the courthouse? Did that violence still run in his blood?

The shadow of the Confederate statue lengthened on the sidewalk as the man spoke again. "You'd better leave town. We don't like your kind around here."

Not looking for more trouble, he, his wife, and the couple they were traveling with left the sleepy mountain town of Hillsville, Virginia, to travel on.

The narrator of this story was my own grandfather. This telling of the Hillsville story intrigued me not only because it possibly involved my own family, but also because of the overt division of the town, shown in their reaction to a stranger who merely looked like an Allen family member. Immediately after my Papa told me this story, I started doing research. I read Ronald W. Hall's *The Carroll County Courthouse Tragedy*. I even made a trip to the town to see the courthouse and visit with Ron. After I wrote a graduate seminar paper (which turned into my doctoral dissertation) on the event, aspects of the shoot-out still stayed with me. Similar to most of Hillsville's citizens, I wanted to know more. Who were the Allens? Why is the town still divided? What further constructions of the shoot-out existed? How has the town healed? But mostly, how has the shoot-out been remembered in different ways? To begin, I had to look to the facts of the story itself.

The Story of the Century

The story of the shoot-out starts with a brawl over a young woman. Brothers Wesley and Sidna Edwards got into a fight during one of their uncle Garland Allen's church services. Wesley had drawn a red ear of corn at a corn shucking earlier in the week and had kissed a girl who already had a boyfriend. Specific details about the fight at the church differ, but the fact stands that a skirmish did break out among the boys at the church house. Wesley was charged with "assault, disturbing public worship with a second count of doing so while intoxicated, attempting to kill William Thomas by aiming and shooting a pistol at him and a fourth one for carrying a concealed pistol with a second count of carrying a concealed blackjack." Sidna Edwards was charged with "disturbing worship, carrying a concealed weapon and felony assault."[2] Carroll County deputy Thomas F. "Pink" Samuels and recently deputized Peter Easter tied the two boys up and chose to drive them past their uncle Floyd's house on their way into Hillsville. Floyd was like a father figure to them; his sister, Alverta, was their mother. Their father had passed, so Floyd looked after the boys. Hillsville locals note that the lawmen took the boys past the house to spite Floyd Allen since the lawmen worked for the local Republican government and Floyd was a Democrat. Accounts again vary as to what happened when Floyd came out of the house. The rumor was that Floyd knocked Samuels in the head with his pistol and freed the boys. As a result, Floyd was charged with "three indictments [. . .] one for rescue of prisoners in custody, one for assault and one for maiming."[3]

On the morning of Thursday, March 14, 1912, Floyd Allen was brought to trial and found guilty of the three charges. After Judge Massie announced the jury's verdict, Floyd stood in the courthouse and uttered the famous words, "Gentlemen, I ain't a-goin'." Immediately, shots rang out in the courthouse, which led to the deaths of five people: the commonwealth attorney, the judge, a jury member, the sheriff, and a female witness. Seven more were wounded. The Allen men immediately fled the scene, some traveling to the nearby mountains and others to the Midwest. However, by September 1912 detectives for the Baldwin–Felts Detective Agency apprehended the rest of the men. The following spring—on Friday, March 28—both Floyd and his son, Claude, were put to death by electrocution in Richmond, Virginia. The rest of the Allen men were pardoned months later.

Prior to the shoot-out, tension had already been building between the Allens and the local government. The Allens' objection to the town's progressivism could have been one of the lead causes of the shoot-out and their trouble with the local government. Wake Forest professor Randal L. Hall explains this point in his article "Justifying Violence: Ninety Years of Remembering a 1912 Courtroom Massacre in Virginia's Blue Ridge Mountains":

> In Carroll County, the Republicans had gained control of local government in the years just after the turn of the century, ending Democratic dominance there. At the state level, though, Virginia remained firmly in the hands of the Democratic party, and the state government had adopted some modernizing measures in the first decade of the twentieth century, some as part of a revision of the state constitution that passed in 1902. A significant aspect of the new constitution was the strengthening of state control over local courts. Beginning in 1904 the judge for Carroll County's criminal court came from outside the county and held in Hillsville periodically as part of a circuit.[4]

In Hall's essay, he further argues that the Allen family represented an escape from progressive government. He states that Governor Mann "emphasized that the Allens had done much more than commit murder; they had challenged the allegiance to rationality and social order by which Progressives expected to guide Virginia to a bright and stable future."[5] Thus, the Allens stood not only as small-town entrepreneurs, but also as social radicals as well. Their way of living encroached on the town's progressive aspirations. Not only were they considered criminal outlaws in the sense that they often broke the law and ended up in jail, but they were political outlaws as well because they believed in an isolationist political system that existed outside of the system that operated in their small town of Hillsville. They wanted to create their own lives without the hinderance of government getting in the way.

Creation of Appalachia as a Region

This story is couched within the numerous and changing definitions of the Appalachian region. Past scholarship on Appalachia defines it as a region, an ethnicity, or a shared set of cultural practices and representations. To understand how rhetorical work can navigate these definitions and what it reveals about Appalachia, we have to first take a look at what these categories are and who created these definitions.

Appalachia as a region was first described in the early 1920s. These assumptions sprouted from late-nineteenth-century travel writers who came to the region to write and vacation, creating the first stereotypes about the region in their writings. Later, historians such as Harry Caudill, Jack Weller, Horace Kephart, and John C. Campbell wanted to define the region based on the culture that existed within the geographical confines of the region. They separated the region from the rest of the country as exceptional. Within their disciplines, these scholars distinguished the daily life of "the mountaineer" and his peculiar, pioneer way of living.

After this definition, Appalachia became a study of a different culture that was based often on Scots Irish descent and exceptionalism, ignoring the political and financial oppression that often happened in the mountains. Scholars such as Allen Batteau, David E. Whisnant, and James Moffett studied the region as one that stood distinct from the rest of the country. It was no longer defined geographically (but that still was a major component), but instead the culture of the region was looked at closely, mostly using case studies (Whisnant and Moffett) and the development of the regional identity (Batteau). Newer conversations continue to emerge of Appalachia as a global region; however, even contemporary Appalachian Studies scholars tend to create nostalgia for the region much like the earlier historians. Obermiller and Scott point out

> the tendency of some Appalachian studies scholars, artists, and activists to represent Appalachian communities in an ahistorical, idealized fashion that neglects political oppression and economic exploitation within the region's localities. Such a tendency results in a 'reactionary nostalgia' that, at best, does little to address economic inequity and, at worst, is complicit in the perpetuation of such inequity.[6]

The nostalgic musings on the region by these contemporary scholars and the early historians are important because these identities also impact the cultural productions of the shoot-out. Notions of a pioneer America and Appalachia emerge frequently in the media, ballads, and museum portrayals of the event. For example, one museum local to Hillsville, the Harmon Museum, couples the shoot-out with pioneer images of a fireplace and cookware. Similarly, media depictions represent the Allen men as part of a culture that existed in the past.

Depictions of Appalachia continue to occur in the national spotlight. These earlier, poverty-centered depictions of Appalachia continue to be produced as a result of the publication of J. D. Vance's *Hillbilly Elegy: A Memoir of a Family and Culture in Crisis* (2016) and the adaptation of the book into a Netflix film directed by Ron Howard (2020). Both of these renditions received national attention and depend on many of the same stereotypes that the media conveyed in 1912. Instead of the shiftless hillbilly on the porch, these new images contain drug or alcohol addled hillbillies scratching out a living on the mountain. Recently, local writers and scholars from the region have developed their own responses to these abject depictions. Publications such as *Appalachian Reckoning: A Region Responds to* Hillbilly Elegy edited by Anthony Harkins and Meredith McCarroll (2019) and *What You Are Getting Wrong about Appalachia* by Elizabeth Catte (2018) respond directly to Vance's text. In addition, historical texts such as *Ramp Hollow: The Ordeal of Appalachia* by Steve Stoll (2017) and *Hill Women: Finding Family and a Way Forward in the Appalachian Mountains* by Cassie Chambers (2020) take a historic and memoir approach that dictates a more compassionate view of the region. More realistic portrayals are seen in the documentary *Hillbilly* (2018) and the miniseries *Dopesick* (2021). They convey examples of political divides, class, and drug abuse in brutally honest ways. I include these new texts because they serve as examples of reactions to the stereotypes that writers, scholars, and the media have placed upon the region. The media coverage, now and at the time of the shoot-out, often continues to evoke these stereotypical images. The context of the shoot-out was much more complicated than the media depicted. It involved both personal and political conflict on both sides. The men involved were either highly educated or were prominent business owners in the town. (Claude Allen went to business school in Raleigh. J. Sidna Allen had gained his wealth from running a store in Alaska.) They were *not* the gangster or hillbilly personas that the media rendered in its coverage.

A Brief Literature Review

Despite front-page coverage in the *New York Times* until the RMS *Titanic* sank, there has been very little scholarly research done on the 1912 Hillsville, Virginia, courthouse shoot-out. Soon after the shoot-out, several religious pamphlets and novellas were published depicting the Allen men as evil. Some examples are *The Allen Outlaws and Their Career of Crime in the Mountains of Virginia* by Edgar James (1912), *The Allen Gang: Outlaws of the Blue Ridge Mountains: The Greatest Sensation and Boldest Crime of the Twentieth Century: A Graphic and Interesting Account of the Hillsville Tragedy, Moonshiners and Mountaineers' Life in the Mountains of Virginia* by J. J. Reynolds (1912), and *"Gentlemen, I Ain't A-Goin'": The Hillsville Tragedy from the Morning of the Tragedy, through the Courts, to the Cemetery* (1912), which was self-published by Samuel S. Hurt from nearby Wytheville. Both nonfictional and fictional accounts of the shoot-out continue to be published, but without the religious fervor of these initial publications. The play *A Tragedy at Hillsville: A Play in Three Acts* by Ronald J. Larson was published in *Appalachian Journal* in 1979. William Lord published many of the trial transcripts in 1999 in *The Red Ear of Corn*. J. Sidna Allen's granddaughter, Betsy W. Chandler, republished his 1929 memoir in 1999 with her own last chapter titled "Leaving Behind the Hillsville Courthouse Happenings, Recalling Another Era (at your own risk of course!)," illustrating her own distance from the incident.

There was even a rock opera titled *Sid Allen and the Devil's Den: An American Rock Opera* by Tom Harvey that was performed at a reunion of the event in 1997 in Hillsville. Recently, two novels—*No Villains, No Heroes* by Thomas Moore (2012) and *Mountain Justice* by Jerry L. Haynes (2012)—were published that fictionalized the event. In August 2020, Chad Tucker with Fox 8 News, out of Greensboro, North Carolina, released a three-episode podcast called *57 Shots in 90 Seconds* that covers the historical aspects of the shoot-out. Local playwright Frank Levering continues to have his courthouse plays performed in the historic courthouse annually. Because of the centennial of the event, there seems to be a resurgence of fiction about it; however, very few of these texts critically examine exactly how the event is rhetorically constructed in past and present rememberings.

Academic scholarship on the shoot-out is indeed sporadic as well. The Carroll County Historical Society published Ronald W. Hall's (local historian and leading scholar on the event) pivotal text *The Carroll County Courthouse Tragedy: A True Account of the 1912 Gun Battle That Shocked the Nation; Its Causes and the Aftermath* in 1997. However, Peter Aceves's article, "The Hillsville Tragedy in Court Record, Mass Media and Folk Balladry: A Problem in Historical Documentation," in the *Keystone Folklore Quarterly* (1971) analyzes different variations of the "Sidna Allen" and "Claude Allen" ballads. The most recent work was done by historian Randal L. Hall (no relation to Ronald W. Hall) in 2004 in the articles "Constructing Violence: Historical Memory and a 1912 Courtroom Massacre in Virginia's Blue Ridge Mountains" and "A Courtroom Massacre: Politics and Public Sentiment in Progressive-Era Virginia."

Rhetorical Rememberings as Public Memories

Unlike most of the historic and literary scholarship done on the shoot-out, my study will look at particular rhetorical rememberings in media depictions, ballads, plays, and museums, as well as the construction of gender in the retellings. Examining these forms reveals rhetorical decisions that were made for each retelling of the story. I define *rhetorical remembering* as how individuals create public or private artifacts or memories that construct meaning about a public event. These meanings, while attempting to construct the history of the event, depict the creators' own rhetorical approach to the event. In the case of the shoot-out, these approaches construct the Allen men and those involved in several different ways, from the stereotyped hillbilly figures in the media to the empathetic, realistic characters in Frank Levering's plays. These past and contemporary rhetorical rememberings of the shoot-out produce new views of how Appalachia was and continues to be constructed through public memories of the event. Adam H. Domby expands on how these rememberings are not bound by history, but by the cultural needs of those who retell it:

> While neither history nor memory can ever be entirely objective, memory, unlike history is not bound by facts, sources, or evidence. The gap between what actually happened and what society recalls is often a vast chasm. Additionally, memory, both historical and individual, evolves and is not reliant upon research as much as it is upon culture and the needs of the present.[7]

Each remembrance in the media, ballads, plays, and museums evinces the cultural moment or kairos of whomever is creating that remembrance. In other words, it represents the person creating it and the cultural time of creation.

These rhetorical rememberings also address public memory scholarship because they align with three intersections between rhetoric and public memory that Dickinson, Blair, and Ott discuss in *Places of Public Memory*. The first intersection is that "public memory is understood by most, if not all, contemporary scholars as activated by concerns, issues, or anxieties of the present."[8] This definition works well with Hillsville because all of these depictions of the event present the tension and "anxieties" of the past with the creation of the identity of Appalachia. In noticing the recirculation of these materials recently on the anniversary of the event, local newspapers and local playwrights still present anxieties about the region and depend on stereotypes to depict the shoot-out. It's a region that is not like the norm; one where outside media generally depends on gratuitous or feud-based violence to depict the mountains.

The second intersection between public memory and rhetoric is that "public memory is theorized in most scholarship as narrating a common identity, a construction that forwards an at least momentarily definitive articulation of the group."[9] This "group" is the Allen men who participated in the shoot-out. They are "articulated" in many different rememberings; however, we see in newspaper accounts that this "common identity" also represents connotations of Appalachia as represented by the different stereotypical accounts of the Allen men, whereas later rememberings present more realistic, tragic portrayals.

The third intersection is that "[public] memory is typically understood as animated by affect [. . .] [Rather] than representing a fully developed chronicle of the social group's past, public memory embraces event, people, objects and places that it deems worthy of preservation, based on some kind of emotional attachment."[10] This intersection is particularly useful with the shoot-out because this uptake of certain "event[s], people, objects, and places [. . .] worthy of preservation" is evident in how the artifacts reflect the rememberings of the event. These artifacts also coincide with what Dickinson, Blair, and Ott deem "rhetorical resources" that create "public memories."[11] Artifacts and ideas emerge, such as the following: Who does the newspaper frequently mention, and why? Who and what actions do the ballads and plays linger on? How do the museums tell their story of the shoot-out and through what artifacts? How does gender play a role, and why should we look toward that construction of the shoot-out? How do the depictions give us a larger understanding of the nation's conception of Appalachia at the time?

The answers to these questions rely on a deeper understanding of the types of public memories that exist about the shoot-out. John Bodnar explains that "public memory emerges from the intersection of official and vernacular cultural expressions."[12] Vernacular culture depends on the constantly changing personal views and values of a small group of people rather than a larger national community, i.e., the citizens of Hillsville. These views express "what social reality feels like rather than what it should be like."[13] In comparison, official culture "promotes a nationalistic, patriotic culture of the whole that mediates an assortment of vernacular interests."[14] In other words, the official memory entails a documented history that the government or other sanctioned organizers or officials deem true and necessary to record. Vernacular and official histories help us examine these memories in ways that rhetorical study scholars find useful. They allow us to examine the kairos and rhetorical situation of these memorial sites and to analyze how, when, and why they are used.

Engaging with Bodnar's definitions, vernacular histories ask us to participate. They depend on oral narratives (such as the one provided by the curator of Carroll County Historical Society and Museum, Bill Webb) to tell us about the event. These rememberings may ask us to consider the dual sides of the ballads represented by the local government and the Allen family. Or they might ask us to consider the consequences of the shoot-out itself, such as in Frank Levering's plays, which portray an empathetic view of the shoot-out.

Official rememberings tell us how to remember events with limited or no participation. These can be located in newspapers, which recount specific events and describe the initial reactions to the events. News articles often convey the information designated by official news sources. Official rememberings are also found in public memory sites. For example, the Mount Airy Museum of Regional

History contains an exhibit about the shoot-out that requires limited conversation or interaction. Unlike other museums, it constructs a very narrow and linear explanation of the shoot-out, with brief vernacular interruptions and little freedom for anyone to explore other iterations of the narrative.

Both the vernacular and the official rememberings contribute to the development of the shoot-out. These rememberings range from stereotypical depictions of the Allen men to more tragic portrayals. For example, in chapter 1, Floyd Allen is portrayed in the newspapers as an outlaw similar to Jesse James, but in the plays that I discuss in chapter 3, Frank Levering writes him as a mournful, sympathetic character who regrets causing the shoot-out. These rememberings, then, give us a means to understand what DeVoss and Ridolfo describe as the rhetorical velocity of the shoot-out and its circulation at various moments in history. Each of these rememberings illustrate how the shoot-out is "the text" that is "recomposed."[15] The artifacts are retrofitted to serve the purposes of those who use them. Whether they are to provide news and entertainment (in media depictions), to demonstrate a side of the story (through ballads), or to serve as a memorial to those who were killed (as seen in a museum), each artifact illustrates how these materials are used to serve different rhetorical purposes.

In addition to memory scholarship, the latter part of my study includes Lisa Blakenship's idea of rhetorical empathy. This theory is useful because Levering's shoot-out plays allow for a new rhetorical remembering of the event that links it directly to empathy for both sides of the shoot-out. Blankenship links the two ideas, stating, "Empathy, like rhetoric, is an epistemology, a way of knowing and understanding, a complex combination of intention and emotion."[16] Her idea of rhetorical empathy involves a "deliberate attempt to understand an Other *and* the emotions that can result from such attempts."[17] In this case, the "Other" would the Allen family members trying to understand the courthouse's perspective, or vice versa. Blankenship explains that rhetorical empathy changes oneself because of the attempts mentioned above. These ideas of attempted understanding and empathy come to fruition through the emotional performances of the characters in the plays. This is especially evident in Frances Allen, who leaves audience members with a true empathetic feeling for all of the lives lost in the shoot-out. This theory is key to understanding how the narrative moves from a male-centered, or masculine, violent retelling of the shoot-out that only involves the men to a new narrative that involves empathy and healing through the recovered and fictional voices of the women involved in the shoot-out.

Chapter Overviews

The first chapter, "'The Many Untruths': Newspaper Representations of the 1912 Hillsville, Virginia, Courthouse Shoot-Out," focuses on rhetorical representations in media depictions of the event. This chapter establishes three rememberings: violent mountaineer, gangster, and uncolonized other. These appear in front-page articles, editorials, and even in political cartoons drawn about the shoot-out. These initial portrayals demonstrate how the media presented the shoot-out to the public and, in turn, how the public reacted to the shoot-out. The future tropes that cover the shoot-out echo these rememberings.

"Performing Hillsville, Part One: Rhetorical Discourse on the Allen Ballads" examines performances of ballads about the shoot-out that contain many of the stereotypes seen in media depictions. Fitting in the genre of the traditional mountain ballad, "Sidna Allen" and "Claude Allen" depict the two different sides of the shoot-out. They demonstrate the schism that happened in the town and the emotional trauma that is still felt in Hillsville today. "Sidna Allen," however, presents a stereotypical portrayal of the Allen men, whereas "Claude Allen" evokes a sympathetic and tragic remembering.

Much like the sympathetic renderings of "Claude Allen," my third chapter—"Performing Hillsville, Part Two: A Rhetorical Uptake of Frank Levering's Shoot-Out Plays"—illustrates a new portrayal of the shoot-out that includes four "spectacular moments" in the plays that cause empathetic moments of rhetoric to happen with the audience and actors. The chapter starts with an analysis of the historic courthouse where the actors perform the play to illustrate how it is a site of memorial and public memory that evokes the dangerous hillbilly stereotype. This analysis is then contrasted with the play, which evokes empathetic emotions toward the characters involved. These empathetic "spectacular moments" are used to demonstrate the exchange that happens between the play and audience members to create a new retelling that allows for healing.

After a brief analysis of the historic courtroom and the Levering plays, in chapter 4, titled "'Feelings Are Still Very Strong': Sites of Public Memory in Hillsville, Virginia," I look at the vernacular and official histories of the shoot-out in three museums local to Hillsville. These histories demonstrate the values of the communities where they are located and provide epideictic, historical moments as patrons are led through three different constructions and experiences of the shoot-out. These constructions include the vernacular, humanistic views provided by the Carroll County Historical Society and Museum and the official, stereotypical portrayals at the Mount Airy Museum of Regional History. The Carroll County Historical Society and Museum, located at the courthouse where the events occurred, gives a ground zero approach that relies on the guidance of its curator, Bill Webb, to guide patrons through. The Mount Airy Museum of Regional History, on the other hand, attempts to officially place Hillsville in the construction of the Appalachian region. Lastly, the most vernacular museum, the Harmon Museum, asks patrons to construct their own versions of the shoot-out through an assortment of artifacts, ranging from local newspapers to more intimate objects, like Floyd Allen's

Front of the Courthouse, Hillsville, VA. Photograph by author.

saddlebags. Each of these museums demonstrates that the story of the shoot-out continues to influence Hillsville's culture today.

My fifth and last chapter, "'I Wish You Had Not Thought to Come Here': Feminine Silences, Pleas, and Community Rhetorics from the 1912 Hillsville, Virginia, Courthouse Shoot-Out," focuses on giving voice to the women involved in the shoot-out through archival materials, and demonstrates how the women's fictional roles in Levering's plays continue to allow for empathy for both sides. Evoking a memory of resilient silence, the women directly involved with the shoot-out do not want to retell the story. While these archival voices are crucial in understanding the emergence of women's voices in the shoot-out, Levering's plays also provide a fruitful place for recovering these women's voices. Analyzing these voices through the theory of empathetic rhetorics demonstrates how they make a difference in the retelling of the story. Whether they are archival or fictional, the women's voices validate that there is a need to approach the shoot-out in a different way other than the masculine-based violence that has served as the dominant narrative for so long.

These chapters work together to not just retell the story of the shoot-out that happened in the historic courthouse (see Fig. 0.1), but also to analyze the rhetorical rememberings of the cultural artifacts that serve as sites of remembrance. Within these retellings, these rememberings struggle with Appalachian stereotypes; however, they also show the possibility of expansion of scholarship on the shoot-out by including gender through the rhetorical agency and acts of the women in the shoot-out. Analyzing the shoot-out through the use of these rememberings allows not only a return to the tragedy of that rainy day in March, but also a better understanding of the production of memories and stories that evolved from the event.

"The Many Untruths"

Newspaper Representations of the 1912 Hillsville, Virginia, Courthouse Shoot-Out

> And at the day of judgment, I feel confident, those editors and reporters who so inflamed the public against us will be held responsible for the deaths of Floyd and Claude Allen and for the heavy sentences imposed upon the rest of us. More than anything else, the many untruths circulated by the press were responsible for the execution of my brother and nephew.
>
> Sidna Allen in *Memoirs of J. Sidna Allen.*[1]

In the Hillsville, Virginia, courtroom on March 11, 1912, the trial of Floyd Allen finally happened after several continuances. After a few minor tasks in the courtroom and some pleading from Floyd's lawyer and friend, Judge Bolen, Judge Massie stated, "Judge, is there anything further you can do with your case today," to which Bolen replied, "No, sir, I don't reckon there is."[2] Massie then asked Sheriff Lewis Webb to take charge of Floyd Allen. As Webb ambled his way over, Floyd dropped his chair from sitting on two legs, stood up, supposedly put his hand in his jacket pocket, and said "Gentlemen, I ain't a-goin'." What happened after Floyd uttered those words has been speculation for the past 110 years. Nevertheless, the gun fight that broke out continued from the courthouse out into the street, where Floyd was wounded and taken to a hotel across the road. The rest of the Allen men fled and were found later.

Within two days of the shoot-out, coverage started in local and national newspapers. Almost every depiction sensationalized the event and presented readers with a stereotypical view of the Allen men on the front page of their newspapers:

An article dispatched from Richmond, Virginia, was published in the *Richmond Times-Dispatch* on March 15, 1912, under the title "Expecting Death in Discharge of Their Duty, Court Officers Are Shot Down in Cold Blood by Carroll County Desperadoes" with the subheading "Acts of Outlaws Terrorize Town to Point of Paralysis, Citizens Take to Flight and Mothers Carry Children to Places of Safety—No Man Left to Organize Pursuit." It reported the following:

> A Troop of mountain outlaws rode down out of the Blue Ridge to-day [*sic*] to the Carroll county courthouse here and assassinated the judge upon the bench, the prosecutor before the bar and the sheriff at the door while sentence was being pronounced upon Floyd Allen, one of their number. When the crack of the rifles died away only one member of the human fabric of the court—Dexter Goad, the clerk—was alive, and he had been wounded. Jury and onlookers were struck in the fusillade, but none was wounded seriously.[3]

Another report dispatched from Topeka, Kansas, and printed in the *Kansas Baptist Herald* (an African American newspaper) on March 16, 1912, under the title "Mob Wipe Out Court" said:

> In a flame of unprecedented outlawry the entire human fabric of the Carroll county circuit court in session here today was wiped out by assassination. Judge Massie had sentenced Floyd Allen to one year in prison for aiding in the escape of a county prisoner. two [*sic*] of Allen's brothers and several of their friends opened fire with revolvers. Judge Massie fell dead in his place on the bench on the first volley. Then the weapons were turned on Commonwealth Attorney Wm. Foster and he sank to the floor with several bullets in his brain, death being instantaneous.[4]

Dispatched from Roanoke, Virginia, an article titled "Outlaws Slay Judge in Court" appeared in the *New York Times* on March 18, 1912. The article included the following description:

> a troop of twenty mud-splashed mountaineers galloped in with rifles from the surrounding hills early this morning, and in less time than it takes to tell it to the Judge upon the bench, the prosecutor before the bar, and the Sheriff at the door lay dead in the courtroom.[5]

While this writing is entertaining, it is utterly false. The Allens most certainly did not gallop in with rifles nor were there twenty Allen men at the courthouse during the shoot-out. These dispatchers, similar to other reporters at the time, create a narrative that relies on Appalachian stereotypes that were starting to take shape in the nation. In fact, these reporters fed off of each other's articles with the repetition of words like "troop," "human fabric," and "mud-splashed." Their reports may have captivated readers, but these absurd accounts pushed forward the Appalachian stereotypes that we often see today.

The promotion of these stereotypes by journalists rendered a certain rhetorical remembering of Hillsville. These depictions do *not* represent the "true" Hillsville in the mountains of Virginia, but rather one that exists in the folklore and stereotypes of the media uptake of the shoot-out. The creation of this fictional place emerged from visiting reporters who frequented the region. These reporters arrived several days after the event and relied on public witnesses of the shoot-out to construct their stories. The passing down of this information conflated and fictionalized what was reported. These articles brought existing stereotypes and cultural anxieties to bear on the situation in Hillsville, resulting in the perpetuation of those stereotypes rather than an accurate account of the shoot-out.

In addition to the collective memories of the people of Hillsville, journalists also drew on nineteenth-century fictional depictions of Appalachia as an underdeveloped region of the United States. Indeed, Appalachia was once glamorized by fiction writers. Specifically, local-color writers from the lowland South contributed to stereotypical fiction about the mysterious mountaineer. In 1912, the image of the mountaineer was just beginning to emerge from publications like Mary Noailles Murfree's *In the Tennessee Mountains* (1886), William Eleazar Barton's *Life in the Hills of Kentucky* (1890), and Lucy Furman's *Mothering on Perilous* (1913). These writers created overtly lurid or humorous Appalachian figures. They portrayed Appalachia as an exotic land full of lazy mountain characters who feuded, drank moonshine, and rocked on their ramshackle porches all day. Similar to novels about the old South based on the romanticized Sir Walter Scott fiction, the authors of these local-color works exaggerated elements of the characters and the land. As historian Henry Shapiro notes, they were "local color writers [who] set stories of upper-class romance and lower-class passion" in the Southern Appalachian Mountains.[6] These writers constructed their stories out of brief visits to the Appalachian region and usually made Appalachia seem like a foreign, isolated land.

These stereotypical constructions of Appalachia from reporters and fiction writers alike illustrate that the region had become a problem for American society at this time. The year 1912 was the last year of William Howard Taft's presidency, when the United States moved forward from the Progressive Era and shifted into the modern era. In *A Fierce Discontent: The Rise and Fall of the Progressive Movement in America, 1870–1920*, Michael McGerr explains how the movement encouraged the middle class, saying, "Progressivism, the creed of a crusading middle class, offered the promise of utopianism—and generated the inevitable letdown of unrealistic expectations."[7] McGerr continues, "Progressives wanted not only to use the state to regulate the economy; strikingly, they intended nothing less than to transform other Americans, to remark the nation's feuding, polyglot population in their own middle-class image."[8] The rememberings in the newspapers demonstrate the discomfort of nationalist approaches to Appalachia. It was a place that was foreign and did not fit within the progressive, middle-class norms that continued to develop during this time. Thus, the construction of the hillbilly image in the newspapers designates Appalachians as an "other" to "fix" and remold so they can be folded back into the developing national culture. While these progressive, industrial ideas seemed fruitful, they met their demise in the sinking of the RMS *Titanic* in April 1912; however, the danger of the Progressive movement can be seen earlier, with the shoot-out, which occurred in March. While the sinking of the RMS *Titanic* signifies the dangers of industrialism globally, the shoot-out demonstrates the dangers and anxieties of modernism that emerged both nationally and locally. Even regionally, industrialism had a profound impact.

During this time, the long arm of the extractive industry reached far into Appalachia. Logging had already taken over the region, and coal mining began soon after. While the Allens made their money from local stores and exchanges in town, their awareness of the industrial strife in the region had to be known. At the time, clear tension was building between coal miners and mining companies that would end in brutal battles, such as Matewan (May 1920) and the Battle of Blair Mountain (August 1921). However, earlier conflicts arose between industrialists and mountaineers, as Ronald L. Lewis writes in *The Industrialist and the Mountaineer: The Eastham-Thompson Feud and the Struggle for West Virginia's Timber Frontier*:

> The Eastham-Thompson feud demonstrated how the different cultural worlds of nineteenth and the twentieth centuries were imprinted on individual social behavior. Thompson was a northern Yankee, an active Republican, and a corporation man who threatened to alienate the land and resources from the smallholders. Eastham was an ardent Democrat, a former Confederate soldier, and outdoorsman of repute who was admired by the backwoodsmen. Thompson and those who persecuted Eastham on his behalf were agents in the 'wars of incorporation' that were in full stride in the 1890s, transforming society through the aggregation, consolidation, and centralization of power in a national market system buttressed and protected by a new emphasis on property-oriented law and authority[9]

This feud, very different from the famous Hatfield and McCoys, relies on tensions of region, class, and political affiliation. This clash of backwoodsmen versus corporations can be applied to the Allen men, who associated with many of the people who lived outside the town limits of Hillsville. This group of outliers demonstrated their loyalty as they hid some of the Allen men during the manhunt after the shoot-out.

The shoot-out is not only a case study of how national progressivism clashed with the newly developing idea of Appalachian identity against outsiders, like in the Eastham-Thompson feud, but local politics also played a large role in the event. These struggles manifest in how the Allen men struggled against the Republican views of Hillsville (and the rest of the state of Virginia) at the time. In his article, "Constructing Violence: Historical Memory and a 1912 Courtroom Massacre in Virginia's Blue Ridge Mountains," Randal L. Hall writes that the "Republican party maintained an active political opposition, a legacy of the mountain areas' divided feelings about the American Civil War decades earlier."[10] Except for a couple of minor votes, the Allens remained staunch Democrats. The political leanings of the family contributed to much of the turmoil that occurred between them and the local government of Hillsville. Even though they were successful citizens in the community, the stigma of their political opposition remained dominant in their lives until the shoot-out.

Despite these progressive politics, Hillsville was still stereotyped by the public media as a backward Appalachian town that needed to move into modernity. Allen W. Batteau argues that during the turn of the century, Appalachia's construction moved from fictional, nostalgic stereotypes to something more sinister and real.[11] He writes that "Appalachia is no longer an anodyne for the discontents of civilization; instead, it is an embarrassment, a reminder of an imperfect past. Instead of a pristine wilderness affording escape, Appalachia became epitomized by [. . .] sloth and ignorance."[12] In other words, Appalachia was no longer a place of the nostalgic pioneer past, but rather a place of industry, growth, and inevitable violence. Batteau best describes Appalachia's emerging identity, stating, "As Appalachia entered history, it lost its innocence."[13] The innocence of the nineteenth-century travel writers disappeared and was replaced by depictions of industry. People in Appalachian areas reacted to development with violence. They no longer were the ignorant hillbillies who signed over their mineral rights, but rather were starting to understand that they could stand up for their rights. This attitude led to the West Virginia coal mining wars in the 1920s. Congruent with these depictions, mountain violence started to erupt more regularly.

Historian John Williams situates the mountain violence that started with the Civil War and lasted through the mining wars. He states, "Folklorists William Lynwood Montell argues that the violence of the Civil War years trained mountain people in the use of force to settle personal and political disputes, and that these effects lasted through at least two generations."[14] During these generations between the Civil War and the mining wars in West Virginia, the violence in Hillsville erupted as well as many other violent upheavals across the region.

Similar to Hillsville, Breathitt County, Kentucky, also experienced political tensions that ended in violence. In *Bloody Breathitt: Politics and Violence in the Appalachian South*, T. R. C. Hutton writes, "Breathitt County is a place that earned a singular reputation for killing between the Civil War and World War I; *Bloody Breathitt* is the accumulation of information and misinformation this reputation was made from."[15] The media spun tales that contributed to misinformation about Breathitt County. One example comes from a story that appeared in the *Louisville Courier-Journal* on December 3, 1878, where Confederate captain Bill Strong went after Southern sympathizers who were "legitimate game for the devil, who appeared in the person of Captain Bill Strong."[16] Throughout his study, Hutton writes more about the sensationalized images of these men by both local and national media, and it is clear that they are comparable to the images constructed about the shoot-out.

While there is clear sensationalism in the depiction of Breathitt County, what does not happen is reporting that favors one side or the other, which happened in the retellings of the famous Hatfield and McCoy feud. Altina L. Waller, in *Feud, Hatfields, McCoys, and Social Change in Appalachia, 1860–1900,* notes this separation:

> Kentucky papers led by the *Louisville Courier-Journal* vehemently claimed that the McCoys were the victims of the Hatfield "outlaws"; it printed the West Virginia investigator's report of the "law-abiding" Hatfields with the sarcastic title "Innocents at Home," intending to undermine its credibility. This interpretation was also the most popular with other papers across the country. The *Pittsburg Times*, for example, carried stories with such titles as "West Virginia Barbarians," "Crimes of the Hatfields," and "West Virginia's Bad Characters." The *New York World* called it "West Virginia's Vendetta."[17]

Meanwhile West Virginia papers fought back with their own headlines in favor of the McCoys.

Despite this back and forth, the media coverage is consistent with depictions of the shoot-out that evoke images of violent hillbillies. In fact, Waller notes that the *Wheeling Intelligencer,* on January 27, 1888, said that the "result should be the summary hanging of the whole lot," a statement that we'll see later echoed in the media's depiction of the shoot-out.[18]

Much like the shoot-out, though, once the Hatfields were captured, the writers for the *Louisville Courier-Journal* described the men in a different way, as shown in this passage from an article dated February 17, 1888:

> their appearance was very unlike that of the mountaineers who are frequently guests of the United States while attending court here for making moonshine whiskey. Nearly half the crowd wore white shirts, and three of them had collars about

> their unshaven necks: Soft fur hats covered all their heads and there were nine mustaches among the nine prisoners.

After the trial and conviction of the Allen men, these empathetic depictions are similar in both local and national newspapers. However, with the Hatfield and McCoy feud the *New York Times* still said that "it is evident that a strong course of common schools, churches, soap and water, and other civilizing influences is required before these simple children of nature will forbear to kill a man whenever they take a dislike to him," which further upheld the stereotypical depictions of Appalachia.[19] The sensationalism of mountain violence in the media most certainly contributed to its continuation.

Coinciding with the developing identity of Appalachia, the specific media depictions of the shoot-out participate in rhetorical rememberings that portray Appalachian people as dangerous mountaineers or represent them as other. Despite the difference in tone, both of these depictions still contain stereotypical images of the Appalachian mountaineer. These representations of the Allen men are mediated through local and national news media, editorials, and political cartoons evoking rhetorical rememberings that depict three ideas of the Allens: the violent mountaineer outlaw, gangster, and other. These depictions were crucial to the development of the Appalachian identity during the late nineteenth century and led to the common stereotypes of the contemporary, marginalized hillbilly figure today.

"Rude, Unlettered, and Traditionally Lawless": The Noble Mountaineer Turned Violent Hillbilly

The arrival of the media to this mysterious locale and their role within Hillsville had an impact on these rememberings of the shoot-out. Local historian Ronald W. Hall writes about this onset: "By Monday, it was estimated that that [*sic*] some thirty-odd reporters had descended upon Carroll County. Between the detectives and the reporters, hotel rooms were difficult to get and local citizens boarded some of the newsmen."[20] Much like the travel writers of the nineteenth century in Appalachia noted earlier, these writers did *not* do their research and instead relied on the local lore of Hillsville and lore that they created themselves. Hall continues, "Instead, [the reporters] enjoyed the luxuries of the Texas House Hotel and wandered about town, interviewing 'knowledgeable' people and either taking or posing for photographs."[21] These descriptions show how the media conflates the coverage of the shoot-out with a tourist mindset as they take pictures and pose at the various sites where the shoot-out occurred. There is *very little* actual coverage done of the aftermath of the shoot-out. Instead, these reporters were led by locals out into the hills where Claude, J. Sidna, Wesley Edwards, and other Allen men supposedly were hiding. These wild goose chases are brought up frequently in the papers and led to the publication of numerous blatantly fictitious articles. Two examples of inventive reporting that I cover in chapter 5 extensively are articles about a shoot-out at Sidna Allen's house, where his wife, Betty, was killed. The other detailed how Clerk of Court Dexter Goad's daughter helped him reload his gun in the shoot-out. Because of the media hype behind Miss Goad's "heroic" but fictitious action, a medal was struck for her by the governor's wife, and the governor wrote her a letter. While these two incidents seem harmless, the false media representations had a huge influence on the Allen men as they went to trial after the shoot-out.

In "The Recall at Hillsville," the reporter writes that "the people of the Hillsville neighborhood are rude, unlettered, and traditionally lawless."[22] Not only does this reporter stereotype everyone in Hillsville as rude and ignorant, but he also depicts them as taking up their own version of the law: "The mountaineers felt that the prosecution of Allen, for performing an act of friendship in helping a prisoner to escape, was unjustifiable. The court opposed their views and they have made the court feel the 'people's' power."[23] This report gives us quite a negative vision of the town. Meanwhile, the dispatcher from Roanoke mentioned in the previous section explains that Hillsville "lies in the Beaver Dam Valley, four miles from the top of the Blue Ridge Mountains. Across the valley a strip of indigo along the sky on a clear day shows the Alleghenies." Even though these descriptions seem beautiful, the writer continues, saying, "The country is rough, the roads are bad, and at this time of year, with spring thaws, nearly impassable. Illicit stills are said to be many." While the weather and road conditions most certainly are true for a few parts of Appalachia, the inclusion of the moonshine still shows that this writer is most certainly interested in evoking the hillbilly stereotype here, as the stills are "illicit." The fascination with Hillsville as a mysterious Appalachian place preserves its identity as an other in comparison to the rest of the nation.

"Three Killed in Virginia Court": Mountain Gangsters

As news of the shoot-out intensified, media outlets refer to the Allens as not only mountaineers, but also as a "gang." Organized crime was first starting to take its hold in urban areas like Chicago and New York. These articles create another remembering where the mountaineer/hillbilly image merged with the more contemporary image of the urban gangster. In the *New York Times* index for 1912, *gang* is written fifteen times to refer to the Allens in the shoot-out, mostly appearing during the month of the shoot-out itself. During the months surrounding the event, the word was used to depict any sort of organized, premeditated crime.

Correspondents from the *Wall Street Journal* wrote the following: "Three persons, including the judge, were killed by a *gang* in the court house at Hillsville, Virginia, Carroll County."[24] The article continues, saying, "Outbreak occurred when Lloyd [*sic*] Allen, head of the Allen *gang*, had been found guilty of felony by the jury. Members of the gang [. . .] began shooting when the verdict was announced."[25] In fact, these reporters even wrote about how the Allens were supposedly taking a stand against the law:

> Reports have been coming down the mountain all day that the *outlaws* have recruited a big band to their defense. A lawless element, in which the Allens were ringleaders, has ruled the mountains fastnesses for years. There is a saying among revenue officers that every pine tree shelters a moonshine still. A battle between law and crime is sure to draw recruits here.[26]

These details clearly depict the Allen men as participants in a moonshine ring that operates like an urban organized crime gang. According to these newspapers, this criminal behavior entails recruitment from locals and the constant battle between lawmen and the moonshiners. There are even eyewitness accounts that attempt to corroborate with the reporter's gangster imagery:

> Perkins says that he knows the Allen *gang* well. Their territory is about sixteen miles from Hillsville. Near by runs Shooting Creek, which got its name from the number of revenue men who met their death in the neighborhood. Perkins says the Allen *gang* is about the worst in Carroll County, where the 'moonshiners' are the most desperate. 'I know their attitude at a time like this,' said the revenue agent, 'for I have been within an inch of death at their hands.'[27]

While these descriptions have some semblance in truth since Sidna and Floyd were moonshiners, they are exaggerated. Perkins's association with the Allens serves more as a publicity stunt than a factual account. His observations continue the entertaining and lurid qualities of the shoot-out. There were no deaths of revenue men near Hillsville and his contribution is pure speculation. Perkins's depictions and the previous other accounts do not conceive of the mountaineers as European clans, as we see in later newspapers articles (and in later historical texts such as Shapiro and Campbell), but rather as gang members who reside in a changing progressive world.

African American newspapers also depicted this gangster imagery. On March 16, 1912, the *Kansas Baptist Herald*, an African American newspaper based out of Topeka, Kansas, opens with the following dramatics: "In a flame of unprecedented outlawry the entire human fabric of the Carroll county circuit court in session here today was wiped out by assassination."[28] The article makes the shoot-out seem methodic and not a melee of bullets flying like the *New York Times* article describes: "Judge Massie fell dead in his place [. . .] then the weapons were turned on Commonwealth Attorney Wm. Foster and he sank to the floor with several bullets in his brain."[29] In fact, the power of the courtroom remains in the hands of the Allen men as they "backed slowly out of the room holding all pursuers in check at the point of the revolvers."[30] These depictions change the view of the shoot-out as spontaneous to now an organized assassination of the government men. As outlaws, they methodically blow away everyone in their path without remorse. The raw intensity and drama from these news reports is much different than what is portrayed in mainstream accounts.

Additionally, the *Kansas Baptist Herald* is one of the only newspapers to mention the race of the Allen men. The rest of the article reads, "The vicious white men of this country have let the negro alone long enough to form a mob and kill all of the officers of the court. This is merely the beginning of the mob rules being applied to white men."[31] This reaction exploits the assumption that mob rule is forming in the South. Furthermore, instead of actions against a person of color, white Appalachian men are killing each other in the courtroom. No other newspaper accounts of the shoot-out refer to the race of the Allen men except in later accounts, when editorials refer to the Scots-Irish clans that settled in the Appalachians.

No North, No South—All Wild and Woolly West: Political Cartoons of the Gangster Hillbilly and the Focus on Floyd Allen

In addition to the representations in the articles about the shoot-out, media outlets created political cartoons that depict the gangster image and focus on Floyd Allen. These political cartoons contribute to the rhetorical construction of the shoot-out because they present images of how the media and the American public as a whole visually constructed the Allen men. These visuals move beyond the textual descriptions using stereotypical accents and portrayals of the citizens of Hillsville to realistic and cartoonish images of the Allen men, in particular Floyd Allen. The depictions in the *New York Times* during the month of the shoot-out and *Life* magazine are the most productive for this study because of the direct images of gangster violence.

The first political cartoon occurred in the *New York Times* on March 24, 1912. Before this date, Claude surrendered, the Baldwin–Felts detectives found the last of the Allen men, and the portrayal of the Allen men as lawless symbols solidified in national culture. The visual rhetoric of the illustration itself demonstrates how the nation views the shoot-out. Included is a picture of the political cartoon and then a zoomed-in portion of it. See Figs. 1.1 and 1.2.

In the cartoon, the unknown (but more than likely Floyd) Allen man is drawn in a suit with two guns blaring. The sketch *does not* present the traditional hillbilly figure in overalls, straw hat, and with a pipe in his mouth. The man appears to be well-dressed and wearing nice shoes. In *Hillbilly: A Cultural History of an American*

"Impressions of the Passing Show." *New York Times* (March 24, 1912): ProQuest Historical Newspapers: The New York Times pg. SM16.

Icon, Anthony Harkins writes about how the traditional hillbilly stereotype is not yet apparent in films from 1904 to 1920:

> No figures appear with excessively long beards, oversized and tattered hats, granny dresses, bare feet, or any of the other markers of the cartoonish hillbilly that would subsequently be established. Instead, most characters are dressed in ordinary turn-of-the-century clothing with a slightly rural look. Male leads, even ones portraying moonshiners or feudists, often are dressed in suit coats, boots, and even ties.[32]

Harkins's comments support the idea that the identity of the Appalachian hillbilly was still in development in American culture. The artist draws the figure as a violent gangster rather than a comic or dangerous buffoon. He wields two pistols as he ambles through the street. The judge raises his hand as if shot, and the other man, possibly the sheriff or the commonwealth attorney, flees for his life.

The depictions of the Allen man also entertain the public. Conflating the shoot-out with the rising gangster activity in Chicago reveals that this editorial is not only a moment of entertainment, but

IMPRESSIONS OF THE PASSING SHOW
--- By HY. MAYER
New York Times (1857-1922); Mar 24, 1912;
ProQuest Historical Newspapers: The New York Times with Index
pg. SM16

IMPRESSIONS OF THE PASSING SHOW---By HY. MAYER

"Impressions of the Passing Show." *New York Times* (March 24, 1912): ProQuest Historical Newspapers: The New York Times pg. SM16.

also a revocation of the law. An editorial that occurs the next day in the *New York Times* explains as follows:

> In the so-called novels of adventures, men very much like these and equally ready to use knife and pistol according to the dictates of private judgment, cut figures by no means repulsive or absurd and the gentle reader thrills with very much more of sympathy than of horror when men are killed and property stolen without due—or any—process of law. 'They used to do such things' seems to be a sufficient excuse for the heroes of fiction, and of history, too, for that matter, but the Allens have made the grave mistake of living several centuries too late.[33]

Similar to the earlier stereotypes in the written texts, this writer sets apart the lawlessness with a work of fiction. Much like the exploitative and entertaining aspect of the cartoon above, this shooting provides a thrilling moment for the audience similar to adventure novels. Both pieces depict that the Allens still occupy a time that refuses to keep up with progress; they can no longer be a part of modern society.

The society that the Allen men now belong to is part of the "Wild and Woolly West." There is no North and South, as indicated, but only the violence of Appalachia and the West. Both regions are undignified and represented by a violent refusal to adhere to progress. Both images are united by stereotypes, with the cowboy/outlaw figure and the hillbilly figure. In fact, in another editorial dispatched from Charlotte, North Carolina, Floyd is compared to Jesse James by H. C. Thomas, an employ of the Secret Service Department of the government: "Jesse James was a harmless as a Sunday School teacher in comparison with Floyd Allen."[34] While Floyd was well known locally as a quick-tempered man, these stereotypes, again, are used mainly for entertainment. Thomas's statement demonstrates that Floyd is even *more* dangerous than the Western outlaw, a description that makes readers more invested in reading more about his adventures and dangerous character. As we see in the figure in the drawing, he is shooting not only the courthouse, but also the bank robbers in the car holding a bag of money. This drawing reinforces the idea that the West is becoming settled, but Appalachia still remains a lawless region.

In addition to this rather realistic portrayal of the shoot-out in the *New York Times*, another more comic depiction emerges in *Life* magazine on April 4, 1912. It gives a more cartoonish portrayal of the shoot-out, focusing on the killing of the judge:

Similar to the action in the previous cartoon, this sketch continues to participate in the hillbilly gangster remembering. Because of his famous mustache, the figure on the right is likely Floyd Allen. These cartoons transform Floyd into the original shooter, a violent hillbilly to blame for the violence. He has a look of disappointment and rage, evident in his arched eyebrows and his mustached-adorned scowl. He stands, again, wielding a powerful revolver, arm akimbo to show his anger. The bullet from his gun connects to the head of someone who we would assume to be Judge Massie because of his haircut. The judge has his eyes closed and is in the process of falling over. The artist draws an arrow going down from his head to the ground. There is a "crack, crack" from the gun that is reminiscent of contemporary comic books. The artist chose to focus on this scene because of the vast amount of coverage of Judge Massie's death that recognizes him as one of the most powerful figures in the shoot-out. He is depicted as being gunned down by Floyd when in actuality the judge declared that it was Sidna Allen who killed him.

In this cartoon, Floyd blatantly kills Judge Massie at point-blank range. This illustration opposes the earlier, more complicated cartoon by focusing on the violent act itself, instead of placing the Allens in relation to the rest of the nation. These cartoons stand as examples of how the depictions of the Allen men transcend to another rhetorical remembering of the media: the political cartoon. These cartoons reflect both the realistic and cartoonish/stereotypical rememberings of the gangster image used. They show the Allen men as cold-blooded killers, but also as a crudely drawn figures who commit an act of violence.

"He Had Thirteen Bullet Holes in His Body": Creating Rhetorical Floyd Allen as Hillbilly Gangster Stereotype

This construction of Floyd does not stop with these political cartoons, but rather it continues with stereotypical, outlaw depictions. His role is pivotal in the retelling of the shoot-out because it gives the American public a definitive figure to examine and villainize. Descriptions range from local color dialogue, physical features, and Floyd's own boisterous, violent demeanor.

On March 16, in a *New York Times* article titled "Two More Dead in Allen Feud," the reporter clearly creates a local color voice to use for Floyd that participates in the outlaw rhetorical remembering:

> Ole Floyd Allen ain't never been sent to no prison yet [. . .] and there ain't no Jedge [sic] or Sheriff what's a-goin' to send him thar [*sic*] now. The boys fit like hell yesterday and I hope they all will git away. One of them hounds got me, but I'll never go to no prison. The Allens is all fighters. I reckon as how I've been purty free with my gun, and when I gets away I'll be free with it again. The boys'll be acomin' back for me. But if they don't come I'll never go to no prison alive.

Stereotyping is clearly seen here in the use of words such as "fit like hell" and "purty," and through the use of double negatives and the *a*-prefix. This was clearly *not* Floyd's voice, but instead a gross approximation of how the reporter thought mountain people spoke. Much like the nineteenth-century travel writers' treatment of the mountaineer, the reporter has turned Floyd into a caricature complete with stereotypical hillbilly vernacular that mirrors the cartoonish figure in the last political cartoon.

Fictional Floyd also speaks about himself in the third person, which further cements him as a legend in Hillsville and beyond; he now stands as an icon in the memory of this event and as an active member in the rhetorical Hillsville that the media created. His refusal to go to jail reinforces the idea that the Allens were against going to jail. His tendency toward violence against the law also demonstrates his "outlaw" nature. He would rather choose death than jail.

Just a couple days later, on March 18, a Roanoke dispatcher for the *New York Times* described Floyd as "tall and gaunt, much the familiar type of mountaineer [. . .] in his youth he was a fine figure of strength, and even at 50 now, when his reddish brown whiskers are turning to gray, he is no weakling."[35] This article shows Floyd as a strong mountaineer even in his fifties. The writer continued, noting that Floyd's "familiar boast was that he had thirteen bullet holes in his body, and that five of them had been put there by his brothers."[36] This description shows the skirmishes among the Allen men; it depicts them in the media as violent not only to those outside their family, but to themselves as well.

Floyd is described next as *not* a "friendly mountaineer," but rather the type of mountaineer who would appear in the novels of Fox Jr. and Murfree. He (and the rest of the Allens) are threatening and violent. In the *New York Times* article "Outlaws Slay Judge in Court," the dispatcher includes the following testimonial from a law enforcement agent:

> They have planned to kill me more than once, and but for a friendly mountaineer, Floyd Allen would have succeeded when I last went into the mountains after him [. . .] I arrested the Allens, and when the trial came up they threatened to slay all the officers of the court at Greensboro as well as myself, but their scheme was nipped.[37]

The depiction of the agent presents Floyd as a menacing figure who is out to defend his family even in the face of the law and judicial proceedings. It not only constructs a rhetorical Hillsville, but also a rhetorical, stereotypical Floyd that inhabits the fictional place.

"Of Course They Are Not Monsters": The Uncivilized Other in Hillsville

While these descriptions and cartoons of the Allens rhetorically construct a violent hillbilly gangster remembering, another rhetorical remembering emerges that conveys pity for the Allen men as an uncivilized other. They are dangerous, but their actions are because of their culture. Dr. George W. Summers, who was an educator in southwest Virginia at the time of the shoot-out, elaborates on his view of the mountaineer, saying, "Open, frank, and willing to be friendly is the way I have found [the mountaineers], but once wronged they would go any length to wreak revenge upon the one who harmed them."[38] Summers continues, "I have never known an instance where an innocent man suffered at the hands of a Virginia mountaineer. The Hillsville tragedy is beyond conception."[39] These descriptions frame mountaineers as innocent and honest. They live in their own culture and are not violence unless provoked. Summers's comments do not take into consideration the complicated political climate that created the shoot-out; instead, it relies on the "innocence" of mountaineer culture.

Whereas Summers's response to the shoot-out was that of shock, in the article titled "Shoot the Judge" in the *Wall Street Journal* (published the day after "Outlaws Slay Judge in Court" was printed), a separate writer codes the violence as a cultural reaction to the judge's verdict. The correspondence from Boston notes that "when the sudden personal issue confronted him, he swiftly and passionately expressed in the crack of his mountaineer's rifle, his belief in the recall of judges."[40] The act is labeled "a piece of cowardly terrorism," with their victims having "no defense." The use of the "mountaineer's rifle" still evokes the violent mountaineer stereotype;

however, the writer also includes Floyd's belief that he was wronged. The violence is *not* random, but it is a reaction. Unlike Summers's writing, it was a predicable reaction from a culture that is deemed personal rather than political.

The pinnacle of how the public views the Allens and Appalachia as an uncivilized other occurs in an editorial in the *Baltimore Sun*, which states that "There are but two remedies for such a situation as this, and they are education and extermination. With many of the individuals, the latter is the only remedy."[41] While this paper advocates death to ignorant and violent mountaineers, the piece takes a more blatant turn toward race, saying, "Men and races alike, when they defy civilization, must die. The mountaineers of Virginia and Kentucky and North Carolina like the red Indians and the South African Boers, must learn this lesson."[42] This piece demonstrates that there is absolutely no room in progressive society for the violent mountaineer (nor any other people of color, for that matter). The writer groups the Appalachian region into other regions and cultures that needed to be colonized. The way of life in Appalachia does not match up with "civilized" society. There is the option of education, but this writer is clear that that option is not the best. The editorial reveals a reactionary violence to the violence of the shoot-out.

While the *Baltimore Sun* editorial is indeed brash, the article "Of Course They Are Not Monsters" in the *New York Times* demonstrates how the media has been harsh in their treatment of the mountaineer when it says, "several people have apparently resented the unmitigated harshness which has marked most of the comment upon [the Allens'] crime and have protested that the class to which they belong has its virtues as well as its vices and should be understood as well as condemned."[43] While they are uncivilized, this writer further notes that there needs to be a more public understanding of the mountaineer and his culture. Through that understanding, the possibility of a rationale for the shoot-out could be deciphered.

Within this understanding, the public will see "the savage individualism which is the characteristic of every race with an environment as theirs" that renders the Allens as victims of their violent culture.[44] This depiction of the Allen men makes their violence a result of being raised in the mountains. The writer attempts to evoke sympathy for the Allens, shifting the blame for their actions from the individuals to the culture and region where they live.

In addition to the cultural emphasis, the writer gives a paternalistic view of the Allen men:

> Like everybody else, the mountain people are combinations of good and bad. Probably they are, on the whole, more ignorant than vicious. They are the victims of heredity and alcohol, and now that their isolated region has been invaded they must change or perish.[45]

This passage pushes the uncivilized other to include moonshine, along with the inference of inbreeding through the mention of "heredity." These men can't help themselves because of how they were raised. While it isn't clearly stated here, these stereotypes give way to more modern cultural stereotypes of Appalachia.

The subset of breeding under the uncivilized other is seen in another editorial that claims the Allens were a result of their genetic past. In the article "Should Be a Hunt Not a War," the writer states that an "explanation of the Allens and like families [*sic*] troubles lie in heredity."[46] Agreeing with the previous article, this writer elaborates on the rationale behind the Allens' "heredity," saying, "Often spoken of as 'of purest English strain,' they are, in fact, the descendants of criminals and defectives sent over to Virginia while England still got rid of minor offenders by transporting them to her colonies."[47] This passage makes the Allens seem redeemable as members of European ancestry; however, it is the worst ancestry that made them. They are a product of criminals who came to America. This writer suggests that these citizens are an unfortunate part of

America's history. Giving a historical background, the writer continues, "They were driven back into the mountains when a better class or settlers came over in Cromwell's day."[48] The argument that the people of Appalachia were "driven" into the mountains does not give credit to western migration or the migratory patterns of different cultures into the mountains. This genetic addition to the uncivilized other rememberings implies that the mountaineer is prone to violence because of his historical past. Violence is in his blood. The cartoonish and tongue-in-cheek images in the political cartoons are no longer present; instead, the writer depicts the mountaineer as an uncivilized other that needs to be "educated" or "exterminated."

One of the final editorials for this remembering that demonstrates the need for education occurred in June 1912 in *The Chautauquan*. In an attempt to offer solutions for the problem of the uncivilized mountaineer, the writer makes the following observations:

> The trouble is that the mountaineers and the nation have grown apart. The former need more schools, more sympathetic interest in them, more tact in the administration of law and justice, more sweet reasonableness in the enforcement of regulation that the mountaineer cannot understand or finds detrimental. The mountaineers will not tolerate bureaucratic arrogance, a brutal tone, any more than they will tolerate patronage and condescension, but they will respond to spontaneous good will and helpfulness. In the case of the 'Allen gang' the law must, of course, take its rigorous course. Crime must be punished [. . .] but the larger problem of prevention, of reconciliation, of rescue, is the problem, which should appeal to the serious and enlightened citizenship of the country generally.[49]

This article is most certainly concerned with the anxiety of the mountaineer on the present as it notes that they "need more schools" and "more sweet reasonableness in the enforcement of regulation." Mountaineers (and the Allens specifically) become a group who must grasp these concepts in order to operate in a progressive America. Their assimilation is not necessary; instead, patience and cultural awareness from the nation is required to approach this distinct region. As seen in the last sentence, education of this group of people will act as a prevention method so an occurrence like Hillsville won't happen again.

"Judicially Murdered by the State of Virginia over the Protests of More Than 40,000 of Its Citizens": A Rhetorical Turn to Pitying the Allens

While the violent mountaineer, gangster, and uncivilized other rhetorical rememberings work for analyzing the initial responses to the shoot-out, hunt, and capture of the Allen men, another remembering emerges as Floyd and Claude face the death penalty. This remembering portrays tragic figures who face death for the crimes that they committed against the state. Floyd and Claude stood trial and were found guilty despite the alleged 40,000 names that were signed to public petitions. These petitions still reside in Governor Mann's papers in the Library of Virginia archives. In fact, Floyd acknowledges their existence to Claude in the following written statement given in prison:

> I thank the Journal for the fight that they have made to save our lives. I also want to thank the papers in the State who have helped us and who have tried to give the true facts to the people of this and other States. It has been a great comfort to us to see how many people believe in our innocence and have helped us as they have.[50]

The existence of these "papers," i.e., petitions for pardon and not the news media, illustrate the importance of these public memory documents. Despite the pushback from petitions from throughout Virginia, Governor Mann did not pardon Floyd or Claude nor was he even in his office during their execution.

Along with these petitions, the news media often presented tragic and pathetic images of Floyd and Claude despite the stereotypical and uncivilized rhetorical rememberings used earlier. In one account, Floyd is "ready to go" meet his maker "in a half whisper."[51] Floyd's voice here is *much* different than the stereotypical voice that we heard from "Ole Floyd" in previous news stories. Even though the writer presents him as "a stalwart and powerful figure, with beeting [*sic*] brows and bushy, reddish whiskers," Floyd's voice is rendered as pitiful.[52] He has changed from a hardened gunslinger to a convicted criminal headed to his death. While Floyd's voice is heard, Claude's is mostly silent in the media, making it easier for the public to perceive him as the other scapegoat and victim. We see in these media depictions of Floyd and Claude how the public's anxiety has turned from aggression to sympathy. They realize that another two lives will be taken in addition to those killed in the shoot-out.

"Such Is the Power of the Press": Sidna Allen's Commentary on the Media Coverage of the Shoot-Out

In response to the frequent sympathetic media portrayals of Floyd and Claude (and following their deaths), petitions were passed around for Wesley Edwards and J. Sidna Allen, Floyd's brother, after they were tracked down and caught in Des Moines, Iowa. There was a distinct change in the media as the petitions circulated around the state. J. Sidna Allen mentions this change in his memoir, citing two articles that appeared in the *Danville Register* and the *Richmond Evening Dispatch*. Both of these articles argued that since Governor Harry F. Byrd pardoned Friel Allen and Sidna Edwards, J. Sidna and Wesley Edwards should be pardoned as well. J. Sidna Allen writes,

> On April 23, 1926, the daily papers carried a news story to the effect that on the following Thursday, April 29, our friends, led by Attorneys English and Moss, would present our petitions to the Governor. Bankers, business men, clergymen and others accompanied these volunteer legal representatives when they went before the Governor. To their surprise the Governor informed

> them that the pardons would be granted immediately—that there would be no delay whatever in giving us our release.[53]

J. Sidna Allen's statements as well as some of the media of the time show that the public found fault in killing two more men related to the shoot-out. Because of the changed public opinion seen in the *many* petitions sent to the governor, J. Sidna Allen and Wesley Edwards were pardoned.

To address J. Sidna Allen's pardon and the shoot-out itself, F. H. Lamb published *Memoirs of J. Sidna Allen: A True Narrative of What Really Happened at Hillsville, Virginia* in 1929. In the small chapbook, J. Sidna Allen details the shoot-out, his escape, arrest, incarceration, and eventually his pardon; however, he also clearly writes about how journalists constructed his family in the popular media at the time. His response to the media's portrayals of his family gives us a glimpse into how these rhetorical rememberings affected the Allen family. His comments about the press demonstrate how powerful these depictions were not only to readers of these articles, but also to the Allen men who were affected by the interpretations of these violent images. J. Sidna Allen writes,

> Overnight the boss of a courthouse ring of selfish politicians became a brave champion of the law, while those hitherto opposing this courthouse ring sank into the role of villains—such is the power of the press.[54]

J. Sidna Allen's comments imply that the press relied on the depiction of the Allen men as "villains." This stereotype also gives way to a rhetorical Hillsville manned with violent hillbillies. The media had complete control over how the Allen men were portrayed to the public.

J. Sidna Allen elaborates on the power of the press as he writes about how he and his relatives were characterized in the media and how this contributed to the deaths of Floyd and Claude. He writes,

> And at the day of judgment, I feel confident, those editors and reporters who so inflamed the public against us will be held

> responsible for the deaths of Floyd and Claude Allen and for the heavy sentences imposed upon the rest of us. More than anything else, the many untruths circulated by the press were responsible for the execution of my brother and nephew.[55]

The description acknowledges the “many untruths” that reporters created about the shoot-out. This piece of text presents a clear distrust of outside media that was brought to the mountains. While some reporters did come from smaller cities like Roanoke, most came from bigger cities like New York City and Richmond, Virginia. These reporters stayed in hotels during Floyd Allen’s trial and were often regarded as outsiders by locals such as the Allens. While the trial itself was not significant, the shoot-out and man hunt afterward brought dozens more reporters to the area. This distrust is founded by Appalachia’s wariness toward industry in the region—a region where coal and timber barons bamboozled its residents to sell their lands for cheap, as mentioned earlier in this chapter. These concerns were most certainly justified given the twisted portrayals of the Allens and Hillsville in the media.

Not only does J. Sidna Allen blame reporters for the deaths of his brother and nephew, but he also calls them out for portraying the Allen men as cold-blooded killers, saying,

> The news of the shooting spread rapidly, and the blame for it, of course, was laid upon the Allens. We were pictured to the world as having deliberately and cold-blood-edly shot up the court, while those who had actually brought on the fight were held up as heroes.[56]

In other words, journalists used the image of the violent mountaineer to rationalize the killings. The reporters depended on this depiction because they were not present during the shoot-out itself; they could only rely on those who were present to provide an account of the events. J. Sidna Allen disagreed with the news coverage and instead created empathy for his family in his memoir. In his account, he attempts to displace the popular, official remembering, claiming that the vengeance of the Allen men was not the only thing that led to the shoot-out. He humanizes the Allen men and demonstrates how much power the press truly had at this point in history. Their depictions of the men as ruthless outlaws vilified them when, in fact, the identities of the men were much more complicated, spanning from their own personal interests in the shoot-out to the political factions at work as well. However, as we see in the media coverage, these complicated and humanistic descriptions were boiled down to violent hillbilly stereotypes.

Despite these representations, the people of Hillsville were cognizant of how the media represented the town and its residents. Anthony Harkins explores the uptake of the shoot-out with the people of Hillsville in *Hillbilly: A Cultural History of an American Icon.* In the following observation, Harkins writes about William Aspenwall Bradley of *Harper's Magazine* and Bradley's relationship with the shoot-out and the people of Hillsville: "[Bradley] reports that the townspeople remain indignant about the 'flights of fancy in which they [news reporters] indulged in order to create the requisite local color so sadly lacking in reality.'"[57] Despite these representations, the citizens of Hillsville wanted to create their own version for the national media.

Harkins continues, "Bradley thus acknowledges the national media's deliberate distortions of mountain society and the industrial transformation of the region, while perpetuating standard tropes about mountain violence, lawbreaking and backwardness."[58] He acknowledges the town's perceptions that these depictions are indeed false; however, they are still invested: "The townspeople's surprising willingness to discuss the case, akin to the willingness of the Hatfield clan to brandish weapons for newspaper photographers, might also reveal their secret pride in playing a central role in a national media event."[59] The media is falsely representing the town, yet still, residents of Hillsville are proud to have this court case.[60] They know that it's bringing money into the town and providing them with income. While those closely involved stayed silent, as seen with the women I mention later, the rest of the town is happy to guide the press and the detectives on wild goose chases around the mountains to search for the violent outlaws the media created.

The Allens? Hillsville?: The Shoot-Out as Old News

The coverage of the shoot-out moved off the front page as soon as the RMS *Titanic* sank. An editorial in the *New York Times* noted, "The Allens? Hillsville? It requires a small effort to recall who they are, what they did and where, and when recalled, it is hard to realize how recently we were all intensely interested in and excited by what then seemed a wholesale slaughter."[61] These statements show that the interest of the national media had most certainly shifted. Hillsville was no longer a concern. The writer also noted that this "thrilling" event was in actuality a "slaughter." The writer continued, "All that seems a small matter of more intrinsic importance. To nothing except a really great war, perhaps has here been given in modern times so nearly the exclusive attention of so nearly everybody as the loss of the Titanic."[62] Despite the writer's concluding remarks, the circulation of the shoot-out did not end. In fact, the media's narrative of the shoot-out continued, but it was no longer front-page news. The RMS *Titanic* sank on April 12, 1912, and the news coverage in the *New York Times* continues until at least September.

More recent retellings of the event portrayed by the citizens of Hillsville attempt to humanize the participants and reject the news articles. In fact, in one of the local plays by Frank Levering, the article about the fictional killing of Sidna's wife, produces laughter as she states, "Well, I guess they got me."[63] The false reporting and stereotypical imagery in these articles provoked locals to react and tell their own renditions of the shoot-out—ones that still carried many *untruths*, but that gave a more humanistic rather than stereotypical telling of the event.

Performing Hillsville, Part One

Rhetorical Discourse on the Allen Ballads

> Rather, oral histories are constituted anew, recorded and 'saved' through technology in the name of identically and materiality. Though this 'new' archiving is supposedly against loss, doesn't it institute more profoundly than anything the loss of a **different approach to saving** that is not invested in identicality? Doesn't it further undo an understanding of performance as remaining? Do not such practices buttress the phallocentric insistence of the ocularcentric assumption that if it is not visible, or given to documentation or sonic recording, or otherwise 'houseable' within an archive, it is lost, disappeared?[1]
>
> Rebecca Schneider in *Performing Remains: Art and War in Times of Theatrical Reenactment* (author's emphasis)

The media circulation of the shoot-out discussed in the previous chapter addresses the early media stereotypes written by *outsiders* of the region to set the exigence for the response from *insiders* in the region. These insider responses rest in rhetorical acts that were performed soon after the shoot-out and are still being performed over one hundred years later. These artistic performances, in the genres of ballads and plays, are often *not* recorded, as Rebecca Schneider points out in the above epigraph. They are both meant to be performed to a live audience; the balladeers and actors must "let go" of the performance and allow it to circulate in popular culture. While the live transmissions of these performances are limited to audiences today, researchers of the performances must turn to written portions of the ballads and recorded performances of the play. These performances first stand as examples of collective memory of the event as audience members watch or listen to the story being told and carry that remembering with them; however, because the ballads are written down and turned into material artifacts, they now become instances of public memory where audiences can study their rhetorical circulation and how they might change in the retelling of the event. Using collective and public memory scholarship and performance theory, this chapter will analyze the engagement of the performative and written components of the ballads. Specifically, the chapter will examine how the circulation of the "Sidna Allen" ballad continues the outlaw images in the media but how the remembering of the "Claude Allen" ballad creates a new, empathetic remembering that reflects the later depictions of the Allen men in the media. This empathetic remembering paves the way for the sympathetic portrayals that Levering creates in his plays.

An Introduction to Ballads

When listening to traditional mountain ballads, there is no question that they serve as powerful performative acts. The singing of these ballads is one of the most emotional transmissions of music; the ballads are generally sung in a mournful tone without instrumental accompaniment. These performances convey a sense of history and ancestry to the region. Some of the first ballads ever recorded, like "Barbara Allen," convey European ties, whereas local ballads like "Tom Dooley"[2] render local events that happened in the mountains. Ballad singers and collectors find value in this strong sense of history. The distinct style of a given ballad illustrates the personal and regional history imbued in it. For instance, the Hillsville ballads exemplify the clear disruption in the town that created them. They represent the two sides of the shoot-out, one side for the Allens and the other side for the local government. These ballads are tragic because they ask listeners to suffer through the violence and trauma of the shoot-out. Furthermore, with these ballads, listeners are left with little reconciliation about the shoot-out and are merely presented with the two sides.

The ballads about the shoot-out serve as powerful reminders of the rememberings because they present episodic details, such as the characters of the outlaw and the tragic hero, that draw on these rememberings. Indeed, the ballad genre places an emphasis on characterization that shapes the history of the shoot-out in ways that clearly distinguish between the town's side of the story and the Allens' side. The ballad about Sidna Allen focuses on the shoot-out and his escape, while the ballad about Claude Allen dramatizes his death by electrocution. In comparison, "Sidna Allen" evokes the outlaw rhetorical remembering, portraying Sidna as the dangerous mountaineer that we saw in the media, whereas "Claude Allen" depicts Claude as a tragic hero as his girlfriend and mother weep over his grave.

Much like the European ballads that were passed down in the Appalachian Mountains, these stories are told in third person. More than just words that were put to a melody, the two songs convey a vernacular history of the event that entails the historical conflict between the Allen family and the town. "Sidna Allen" and "Claude Allen" expose the political complications of Hillsville at the time of the shoot-out. In the processes of composing, singing, and passing down these ballads, community members have invested in either the town's role or the Allen family's role in the shoot-out.

To analyze these ballads properly, the ballad genre needs to be explained. Ballads were a way for people to pass down fictional and historical stories through a specific European song tradition. Folklorist Roger deV. Renwick defines the complicated features of a ballad as "a song composed in stanzas sung to a repeating tune that recounts a short, usually single-episodic, tale of complication, climax, and resolution."[3] His description here denotes the telling of a tale: a beginning, a middle, and an end. The Hillsville ballads explain what happened at the shoot-out, the escape, and then the incarceration of Sidna and the death of Claude. But they also characterize these two men in certain ways through the telling. Sidna is portrayed as violent, while Claude is pitiful.

While these two rememberings of the shoot-out convey a slight sense of emotion, it does not dwell too much on the sentimental, like folk songs, but instead rests on the actions and characters of the event. The ballads focus on "the leading character" and "[feature] two interacting protagonists to a scene."[4] Each ballad "develops an episode in which action takes place and is concluded, whereas the other folksongs focus on the articulation of feelings, ideas, fantasies and attitudes without utilizing a narrative thread to achieve their ends."[5] According to these observations, the objective of a ballad is storytelling, in opposition to the often first-person, emotionally charged folk song. I. G. Greer, ballad collector and singer, elaborates on the ballad genre by saying,

> The ballad singer doesn't have a trained voice; you'll soon find that out. The trained voice doesn't interpret the ballads. And this is truly an interpretation. The ballad is a story that you sing. It isn't a ballad unless you sing it. It isn't a ballad unless it tells a story. ("Talk at the G.F. Women's Club, Asheville, NC")[6]

Agreeing with Renwick, Greer argues that the ballad *must* be sung and tell a story. He also asserts that the ballad *must* contain third-person narrative and *not* be in the first person, as seen in the Allen ballads. Greer's comments also state that ballad singers and collectors interpret ballads. The use of the rememberings of these ballads is most certainly an interpretation of how to understand their use in popular culture and in the history of the shoot-out. The two ballads present two ways of viewing the sides of the shoot-out.

While interpretations exist, it is also important to understand where these ballads fall in relation to the classifications of the ballad genre. Renwick splits the ballad genre into the following subtypes: broadside, parlor, blues, and the medieval/Child ballad. The broadside ballad was written down and sold for money on the streets. G. Malcolm Law Jr. categorized the broadside ballad into "two logical divisions for the purpose: ballads that originated in the British Isles (Laws 1957), and ballads that were made on this continent" that had to do with "North American experiences."[7] They are generally in first person and concern "regional and occupational groups," such as "logging, ranching, coalmining, seafaring."[8] Parlor and blues ballads are generally in first person (despite Greer's definition) and are usually played on the piano and the guitar or banjo. These ballads contained moral tales that often paralleled the temperance movement. The classification and specifications of the ballad genre are important because these details clearly indicate that the "Sidna Allen" ballad fits into the broadside ballad format, whereas "Claude Allen" is most certainly a parlor ballad because of its moralistic nature. They are *not* designated as folk songs, which are songs that rely on feelings. Rather, ballads rely on the story itself. The Hillsville ballads tell a story that is *distinctly* Appalachian. The singers invest their story in a narrative that includes hillbillies, mountains, and a sensationalized plotline that is reminiscent of those found in the earlier media depictions.

Lacking the materiality of the newspapers, these ballads are difficult to study because much of their power rests in the performance itself; however, performance theorist Diana Taylor argues that it is crucial to study the materiality of these genres as well. She writes, "The rift, I submit, does not lie between the written and spoken word, but between the *archive* of supposedly enduring materials (i.e., texts, documents, buildings, bones) and the so-called ephemeral *repertoire* of embodied practice/knowledge (i.e., spoken language, dance, sports, ritual)."[9] Taylor's comments suggest that the materiality or archiving of these performance materials is worth studying. The collection of ballads must be studied in written form because the temporality of oral transmission is tougher to analyze, especially since the ballads are so infrequently sang today. While studying the written variants of these ballads does disrupt the oral transmission of the ballad and makes it materialistic, it is the only possible way to study them.

Remembering the Ballads: Collective and Public Memories of the Shoot-Out

The transition from the oral to the written form of the ballads also allows these rememberings to stand as pieces of collective memory and public memory as they come from vernacular, oral rememberings of the ballads to written down pieces of public memory for all audiences to access. Public memory scholars prove helpful in understanding this transition from one form to the other. Edward Casey defines *collective memory* in *Framing Public* as follows:

> [Collective memory involves] circumstances in which different persons, not necessarily known to each other at all, nevertheless recall the same event—again, each in her own way. This is a case of remembering neither individually in isolation from others nor in the company of others with whom one is acquainted but *severally* [. . .] All that matters is commonality of content [. . .] Not the experience but the focus—amounting to a monothetic obsession—is what is shared in collective memory.[10]

From this definition, we can see how these recollections of the event can serve as examples of a specific kind of collective memory. Collective memory must occur first before an artifact of public memory can be established. This definition fits well with the development of the Hillsville ballads, as there are *numerous* variations of these ballads; however, they all maintain the same basic plot, characterization, and resolution. A ballad remains vernacular rather than official because it is not materialized or written down. Rather, it exists orally as each balladeer sings it. It exists only while it is transmitted from the singer's mouth to the audience's ears. It is *not* memorialized on paper to be studied.

However, when ballads are collected and written down, something happens to their circulation. The genre changes as words are transcribed. For example, the name Sidna was changed to Sidney in mountain vernacular. In addition to the name change, various local vernacular words would often change as the ballads were collected. Rhetorical decisions affect how a ballad is constructed in its written form. Meanings are lost, but new ones are incorporated into the new construction of the artifact. These objects become official as they are written down to be studied by folklorists and curators. In *Places of Public Memory* Blair, Dickinson, and Ott explain how documents operate as they move from collective to public memory:

> We have chosen to use the designator "public" memory here, because of rhetoric's emphasis upon concepts of publicity [. . .] we believe, because "public" situates shared memory where [. . .] in constituted audiences, positioned in some kind of relationship of mutuality that implicates their common interests, investments, or destinies, with profound political implications.[11]

Memory here is shared by its constituents and is made concrete in some sort of artifact that is made public, i.e., the publication of the ballads. These ballads can now be circulated more widely than just to those who listen to the ballad singer. The transcribing of the verses has "profound political implications," not only because it shows the political slants of each ballad, but also because the ballads no longer belong only to those who recite them. The ballads also belong to those who can read them from the page.[12] They no longer are passed down from family member to family member, but rather circulate outside the region, ready to be taken up by anyone who can read and study them. The crux of this argument is that the rhetorical constructions of these ballads are now available to be analyzed in full.

The material construction of the ballads also gave way to the monetary production of them from music agencies, including Henry Whitter for Okeh Records in 1924, Hobart Smith, and Clarence Ashley, among other old-time musicians. Interestingly, Ernest "Pop" Stoneman, a popular singer at the same time as Whitter, claims to have written the ballads. In his book on the singing Stoneman family, Ivan Tribe explains, "Ernest [. . .] later told his children about seeing a posse search for the Allens while he [Ernest] hid in a tree."[13] Despite these recordings and local stories, the circulation of the ballads now exists outside of a person-to-person network. In addition to being performed, they can be studied by folklorists and musicologist.

Peter Aceves's (aka Peter Narváez) article "The Hillsville Tragedy in Court Record, Mass Media and Folk Balladry: A Problem in Historical Documentation" demonstrates what happens when folklorists and musicologists collect and study these Hillsville ballads. He writes about the archetypes in the ballads that he describes as "a grouping of the most common traits of a particular oral tradition, i.e., a lumping of the most stable elements of a ballad over a given period of time."[14] By grouping the variants together and boiling down the essential plot points, Aceves creates a larger memorial landscape because he takes the public memory artifacts and then sees how they all fit together. These "stable elements" are basically the main plotlines of each ballad. These archetypical groupings allow readers "to analyze general social attitudes and ideas toward an event, the historian must stress common denominators regardless of what kind of documentation he utilizes."[15] By grouping these actions together, they show how the "social attitudes" surface. Providing that the summative nature of these groupings will leave out some minor details in particular ballads, these archetypes provide an easier way to closely analyze the structure and narrative of the ballads.

Each of these groupings that Aceves has put together exists from the variants of the ballads. Even though they contain thematic features, there are still small distinctions among the ballad variants. For example, in variant 9 of "Claude Allen," the reference to his grave is "Way up on that old, high mountain." In variant 10, the singer notes that it is "Away up there on that cold mountain."[16] Even though these changes are small, they are crucial to the telling of the story and the integrity of the singer. The difference here is that the "high mountain" does not present the loneliness and despair of the "cold mountain." The singer makes a rhetorical decision to recite the ballad in a certain way to depict a certain emotion.

The way that the ballad is constructed denotes the place where it is from. As Aceves notes, "all available song texts have been traced to the southern Appalachian region."[17] While each of these variants is fascinating to study, it is not the scope of this project to go into close analysis of each one; instead, this study will look at particular points in the ballads where the bifurcation of the town and the Allens occur in "Sidna Allen" and "Claude Allen." These places in the ballads demonstrate the schism that still remains in the town. It is a fissure that the Levering plays attempt to heal. While citing from a few variations for textual support, this analysis will demonstrate how the development of the plot of the ballad contributed to the political connotations. Before each analysis, a short biography will introduce Claude and Sidna to explain their roles in the shoot-out. These biographies are meant to disrupt the political leanings of the two ballads. They present what history gives us about these two men; these glimpses of reality are meant to offer assemblages of truth amid the fictional nature and sensationalism of the ballads themselves.

"The Story about a Cruel Mountaineer": Sidna Allen's Ballad

Jeremiah Sidna Allen was Floyd's second brother (brothers Jack and Garland came after) born on July 19, 1866. After having financial success in the Yukon after the gold strike, he returned to Hillsville to run a general store.[18] His reputation in Hillsville was that of a business entrepreneur; however, he, like Floyd, was called upon often to maintain peace in the mountains. In the article "Outlaw Once an Officer," which appeared in the *New York Times* on March 17, 1912, we see a violent side of Sidna: "when the Carolina, Clinchfield, & Ohio Railroad was built several years ago the contractors had continual trouble with the men on the work. As regular as payday came all of the men would get drunk and then would follow gambling and shooting for days."[19] Sidna was hired because he "knew the habits of the mountaineers" and was a "greater bully than they."[20] We see a hardness in how Sidna is revealed. He means business (pun intended) but is also not afraid to commit violence to keep the men in line. Before the shoot-out, Sidna built an elaborate Victorian home off of Highway 52 on the way to Hillsville. He and his family only lived there for eleven months before the shoot-out happened and the house was "attached" to the trial and lost. Sidna was captured in Des Moines, Iowa, with his nephew Wesley Edwards on September 14, 1912, and was pardoned from his prison sentence on April 20, 1926, after serving fourteen years.[21] These descriptions of Sidna are important, as the ballad continues to participate in the outlaw rhetorical rememberings that the newspaper writers constructed.

"Sidney Allen,"[22] variant 15, starts with an invocation to the audience: "Come all you people if you want to hear, / The story about a cruel mountaineer. / Sidney Allen was the villain's name, / At Hillsville courthouse he won his fame."[23] Three variations call him a "brave, famous or truehearted mountaineer," whereas six variants call him a "cruel mountaineer and a villain, bilious man, prisoner, rounder."[24] These attributes portray Sidna both as a mountaineer and as a villain. He exists here as a dual representation of a pioneer and a dangerous hillbilly figure.

Sidna's rash actions in the ballad contribute to his depiction as the violent mountaineer, which is consistent with the image in the outlaw rhetorical remembering. In the ballad itself, however, inconsistencies in the variations demonstrate that the mountaineer could be Floyd *or* Sidna approaching the bench. While it was Floyd's trial that instigated the shoot-out, Sidna was on the docket that day for a counterfeit charge (he was later acquitted after his pardon). Despite why he was there, several variants still state he "mounted to the bar with his pistol in his hand / And sent Judge Massie to the Promised Land."[25] When Judge Massie is shot, we don't get a violent image, but merely that Sidna "sent [him] to the Promised Land."

Soon after the murder of the judge and Sheriff Webb, the variants from Galax and Eries in Virginia include stanzas about Clerk of Court Dexter Goad. The inclusion of Goad further demonstrates the violent mountaineer rhetorical remembering because Goad was known to have drama with the Allen family. Floyd considered him his mortal enemy, which was well known not only throughout Hillsville, but in the surrounding area of Galax, Mount Airy, and Cana. Goad's presence is important here because it continues the entertainment value of the feud and further demonstrates the political division of the town. Collected from Galax, Virginia, variant 13 states,

> Then Deck Goad says "it's a pretty hot place,"
> When a brave mountaineer stared right in the face
> He mounted through the window and these words that he said
> "In a moment later and we'll all be dead"[26]

Generally, these lines are given to Sheriff Webb, who is killed shortly after. It is important that these words are given to Goad, because this act demonstrates that he not only lives after the shoot-out but is also included in the narrative. His voice is preserved in the oral narrative of the story, much like the Allen men. The next stanza continues,

> Dextry Goad, he mounted through the window
> Dextry Goad, he landed in the mud,
> Dextry Goad he mounted through the window
> Cause the fatal feeble man all had covered in blood[27]

While repetition is obviously evident here, it's also important to see Goad fleeing the courthouse. In addition, Goad is a "fatal feeble man all [. . .] covered in blood." The ballads use of these words preserve the fact that Goad was ill, humanizing him, unlike the stereotypical description of Sidna. Despite his condition, the local government side *did* corroborate with Goad, so his inclusion is evidence of this ballad's slant against the Allens; while Sidna is referred to as "brave," he is still brutally violent. It's also worth mentioning that Goad lived through the shoot-out to become a successful lawyer in Hillsville. His inclusion here demonstrates that the Allen men were not the only men to be memorialized in the ballads. The rhetorical remembering here includes not only the violent mountaineers but also those who suffered during the tragedy.

Next, variant 15 presents the local community working with Sidna to help him hide out before his journey west: "Sidney mounted to his poney and away he did ride; / His friends and nephews were riding by his side; / They all shook hands and swore they would hang / Before they'd give up to the ball and chain."[28] This depiction describes Sidna fleeing from the courthouse but also alludes to his family and neighborly connections. Saying how they "all shook hands" reveals a sense of honor and loyalty to one another. They refuse to give Sidna up to the law, and they stick together as a band of outlaws, similar to the description of the Allen gang in the media coverage and many of the museums.

Lastly, these variations of "Sidna Allen" leave listeners with a semblance of pity for Sidna as he is convicted and his children and wife look on, saying, "Oh Lord, don't take papa away."[29] These descriptions still participate in the outlaw image, but Sidna is humanized as a father and husband. However, justice is still warranted for the violent mountaineer as "The people gathered from far and near / To See Sidney sentenced to the electric chair; / But to their great surprise the judge he said: / 'He's going to the penitentiary instead.'"[30]

Historically, Sidna's trial was watched by many in the community. To see that he was convicted to a prison sentence was a surprise to most, considering that Floyd and Claude had already been put to death. All but three of the ballads that Aceves collected stop at Sidna going to prison. Variants from Galax and Eries in Virginia include Sidna riding back from the courthouse to Galax. Variant 24 (from an undisclosed location) actually includes Sidna's pardon, but with an invocation at the end like in "Claude Allen": "Now, this, friends, is the story, of Sydna Allen's case, / We all may seek vain glory but find, instead, disgrace! / But if we could remember before it is too late, / We'd never have to suffer for Sydna Allen's fate."[31] While these outliers are important to recognize, the majority of the ballads stop at his incarceration. The deed is done, and Sidna pays for his crimes. From the town's perspective, Sidna has paid his due for his crimes (although some locals still think that he should have carried out his full term). The murder of the victims has been justified by his prison sentence.

"Poor Claude Was Young and Very Handsome": Claude Allen's Ballad

Claude was the youngest son of Floyd Allen and Cornelia Frances Edwards Allen. Claude, educated in Hillsville, then

> went to the Draughon's Business College in Raleigh, North Carolina where he studied typing and shorthand. After graduation, rather than pursuing a career, he came home to help his father farm the land and help care for his mother who was by then in poor health and nearly an invalid.[32]

It is significant that the media did *not* comment on any of Claude's education; instead, reporters depicted him as an outlaw figure who defended his father during the shoot-out. Claude was twenty-two when the event took place. He and his father were put to death on

March 28, 1913, in Richmond, Virginia. Many of the people in the town of Hillsville saw Claude's death as tragic. Sidna Allen explained that there was even a medal that the ladies of Southwest Virginia made for him stating, "For Bravery in Defending his Father."[33]

Sidna Allen continued to declare Claude's bravery when he said, "the brave boy has long been dead but his memory is still fresh in the hearts of many of his friends. An unfortunate victim of circumstances, his life was demanded of him for defending his father."[34] After the bodies were lowered into the ground, a marker was placed on the graves that stated, "Sacred to the Memory of Claude S. Allen and his Father Who was judicially murdered in the Va. Penitentiary March 28, 1913 by order of the Governor of the State over the protest of 100000 Citizens of the State of Va. Placed here by a friend and citizen of Va."[35] Interestingly, this marker was immediately removed after Governor Mann threatened whoever cast it and placed it there with criminal libel. According to an Allen family member, the marker is still with the family and "being used to honor the dead today."[36]

This brief biography of Claude is important to consider because of the way that the ballad casts him in a compassionate light. The ballad presents a new humanistic rhetorical remembering of the Allens, unlike the stereotypical ones depicted in the newspapers and in Sidna's ballad. Claude's ballad is most certainly a parlor ballad that conveys moral reasoning with a mournful tone, evoking feelings of sympathy for Claude for defending his father. The beginning of variant 1 introduces the audience to Claude's death with "Claude Allen and his dear old Father / Have met their fatal doom at last."[37] These lines demonstrate a familiarity between Floyd and Claude. The use of the word *doom* showcases the severity of the men's deaths. Most variants end the first stanza with "Their friends are glad, their trouble is over, And hope their souls are now at rest."[38] These lines offer an ending to the shoot-out and imply that these characters found peace. Even though peace is found, however, variants 1 and 8.2 of the ballad continue to describe Claude as "young," "very handsome," and "tall."[39] Next, the ballad contains "hope" for Claude because of the various petitions that were sent to Governor Mann from across the state. Currently housed in his papers in the Library of Virginia, these petitions beg the governor to pardon Claude. The inclusion of them in this ballad is crucial because it characterizes Claude as a victim of circumstance and argues that the shoot-out was not his fault. Interestingly, the ballads vacillate about the pardon; sometimes it applies to only Claude, and sometimes it applies to both he and his father.

Nonetheless, Governor Mann does *not* pardon either man, ending in both Floyd's and Claude's deaths by the State of Virginia. In this ballad, we see their deaths as mournful and regrettable, unlike the harsh descriptions of Sidna in the other ballad. Variant 1 of the ballad reads, "But the Governor being so hard hearted, / And caring not what their friends might say, / He gently took his sweet life from him, / And now in the cold grave his body lay."[40] In almost *all* the variants, this stanza is repeated word for word (although *lay* sometimes is replaced with *in clay*). The stanza conveys a sense of retaliatory justice for those in favor of the court. Governor Mann is not depicted as sympathetic to Claude in any way and, in fact, he ignored the petitions that came to his office. According to his comments in the archives in the Library of Virginia, he was adamant that Claude and Floyd were guilty of the crime, and he was out of town during the executions. The stanza, again, conveys sympathy for Claude against the local and state government.

After Claude has been convicted (and presumably killed) in the ballad, we get displays of mournfulness from his girlfriend, Nellie, and his mother, Frances. These depictions humanize Claude, unlike his uncle Sidna. In these sections and in variant 1, the women in Claude's life are showcased as he "had a pretty sweetheart, / who mourns for the loss of the one she loved, / She hopes to meet beyond life's river, / That fair young face in Heaven above."[41] This stanza demonstrates a Christian's view of Nellie meeting Claude in the afterlife. In fact, in variant 2, collected in 1917 in Rusk, North Carolina, Nellie returns at the end of the ballad: "His sweetheart must have been sad-hearted / When she saw poor Claud lying still and cold. / Down on her knees she wept beside him, / And prayed to God to save his soul."[42] Again, we see a Christian plea for Claude's soul to be admitted to the afterlife. There was talk about engagement, but their love was only to be remembered in ballads like this one.

The other lament that occurs in variant 8.1 is for Claude's mother, Frances, who is depicted in the following lines: "Claude's mother's tears were gently flowing / All for the one she loved so dear / it seemed no one could tell her troubles / It seemed no one could tell but her."[43] She is also mentioned in the next stanza in variant 8.2: "How sad, how sad, to think of killing / A man all in his useful years / A-leaving his old mother weeping / And all his friends in bitter tears."[44] Both of these depict Frances as a grief-stricken mother. It most certainly evokes feelings of sympathy for Claude and his family; similar depictions of Frances appear in the Levering plays and media portrayals of her. These depictions further humanize the tragic nature of the shoot-out and reinforce the idea that Claude is a tragic hero who died because of violence.

What is not in the ballad is Claude's trial and conviction for his participation in the shoot-out. He carried a gun to the courthouse, whereas his father did *not*. What the ballad presents is most definitely a one-sided view of Claude and his family, a view that depicts him sympathetically for the Allen side of the shoot-out. Leaving out these details helps evoke a sense of pity for Claude. While he is not depicted as fulfilling a sense of duty like the government officials, his justification was to defend his father. The effect of the shoot-out is not found on him, but in his loss of life. Variant 8 verifies that

"Claud Allen was honored with a gold medal / For taking his dear father's part. / He told them all when he was gone / To give it to his dear sweetheart."[45] The medal here plays a role in him defending his father's honor (which is actually stated on the medal) and bringing in Nellie again for more sympathy. In addition, in the people's lament in variant 6, we see the presentation of Claude's grave: "High upon lonely mountain / Poor Claud sleeps beneath the clay. / No one can hear his words of mercy / Nor see his face till the Judgement Day."[46] This lament gives a graphic portrayal of Claude in his grave on the mountainside (which, geographically, is true). Christianity is evoked, and Claude pleads for redemption from the grave.

The ending of this ballad is indeed moral, serving as a warning to young men to avoid danger. It not only serves as a warning, but also deflects all conviction and Claude's control over the situation. The phrasing is appropriate for the moralistic parlor ballad in that it retains the moral at the end, but it also represents the sympathy for the Allen side of the shoot-out. While standing as a memorial to Claude, this ballad also pushes for nonviolence among the people of Appalachia unless they want an "awful debt to pay." The moral is that even if they are defending their families, they, too, could end up like Claude.

Shoot-Out or Massacre?: Political Exigence in the Ballads

These ballads demonstrate the divisive attitudes that still resonate within the town. "Sidna Allen" represents the violent mountaineer, while "Claude Allen" depicts sympathy and tragedy. These rememberings show the fissure that is still felt in the town, one that the media helped create and perpetuate. It is even evident in which ballad a singer chooses to perform. Aceves (aka Peter Narváez) addresses the politics surrounding the ballads:

> The ballads of "Claude Allen" and "Sidney Allen" reveal this political conflict regarding the incident because of all twenty-one variants considered *no one informant was reported as having offered both ballads to a collector*. That is, since both songs have been in oral circulation simultaneously, it would seem that carriers of oral tradition possessing strong pro or con feelings toward the defendants and their political affiliations have chosen to sing one song or another and not both.[47]

These statements show that each singer makes a deliberate decision when choosing which ballad to perform. If the singer memorizes and performs "Claude Allen," then the singer favors the Allen side of the shoot-out; if a singer chooses "Sidney Allen," then the singer supports the town's side of the shoot-out. What's Aceves doesn't mention here is audience. Clearly though, the singer would *not* perform "Claude Allen" to an audience of people who sympathize with the town. Artist performativity and rhetorical audience serves as a critical part of this rhetorical remembering of the shoot-out.

"Those Ballads Aren't Really Sung Much": Lack of Reception of the Ballads by the Community

In my research I have asked several community members and local historians if these ballads continue to be recited. The answers have been predominately no; however, this answer is a bit more complicated. Being an older genre of music, ballad recitations only occur in small local groups or at academic conferences, such as at gatherings of the American Folklore Society or the Appalachian Studies Association. In these academic circles, ballad collectors and scholars gather to swap ballads and tell stories about who and where the ballads come from. From my experience, I have seldom heard the 1912 Hillsville, Virginia, courthouse shoot-out brought up. However, when questioned about the ballads, several members of the Hillsville community did not even know about the ballads, but they brought up recent songs that local songwriters wrote about the shoot-out.[48]

Despite the absence of the ballads in the local and academic communities, these portrayals of the Allen family demonstrate that this event is still an important part of Hillsville's public and constructed memory that depends on media depictions of the shoot-out. The ballads demonstrate a clear disruption between the brutal violence of the hillbilly figure and opposes that stereotype with the sympathetic penance of Claude Allen. Despite either portrayal, these ballads still portray the Allen men as figures who rebelled against the society in which they lived. Aceves writes that "Claude Allen"

> exhibits antagonisms toward government and law, while ["Sidney Allen"] seems to place ultimate faith in those same institutions. Consequently, the Hillsville tragedy may be viewed as having elicited the oral responses of a society whose values were in a state of transition from the individualism and cooperative spirit of the frontier to the social ethic of twentieth century bureaucratic middle class America.[49]

Clearly from his description, Aceves asserts the use of these ballads in how they show the disruption of the town to the rest of the nation; however, I would argue that the ballads are songs that continue the fissure that erupted with the shoot-out. The tension is still palpable in the town despite the lack of recitation of the ballads. Hillsville residents, however, did find a way to depict the event and heal this fissure. During the centennial celebration of the event, local Hillsville community member Frank Levering wrote four plays about the event. These plays most certainly don't exploit the event, but rather demonstrate a way that the citizens of Hillsville (and the descendants of those involved in the shoot-out) found a way to return to the event with healing instead of the fracturing duality of the ballads.

Performing Hillsville, Part Two

Rhetorical Uptake of Frank Levering's Shoot-Out Plays

> What do you want from me now [. . .] once ain't enough for you [. . .] greedy for guns and blood [. . .] you want to see folks shot, dead. That's what you're here for, trouble.
>
> Frances Allen in *Thunder in the Hills*[1]

Whereas the ballads offer little reconciliation, Frank Levering's plays, performed from 2012 to 2019 (the 2020 performance was canceled because of the pandemic), elaborate on the tragic aspect of the shoot-out. The years between the shoot-out and the present provided some time for the town to come together and remember the event through Levering's plays in the historic courthouse where the shoot-out took place. Healing in Hillsville is different than in other regions of the South and Appalachia. In John Smith's section on "Trauma" in *Keywords for Southern Studies,* he focuses on how the lowland South's definition of *trauma* focuses on the South's loss in the Civil War, race, and ethnicity.[2] In Appalachia, much of the historical healing ties into the history of the region, in particular the exploitation of extractive industry. In "The Ethics of Memory: Commemorating Disasters in an Age of Risk," Tom Bowers analyzes the rhetoric of the trauma and healing that came out of the Buffalo Creek disaster, where a coal dam broke and flooded the town, killing 125 residents, injuring 1,100, and leaving 4,000 homeless.[3] However, we see that the trauma in Hillsville falls in between these two definitions; it is not only tied to the political schism in the town, but also to the trauma of the shoot-out. The media frenzy displays this exploitation and stereotyping of the trauma by outsiders, while the ballads in the previous chapter demonstrate how the schism occurs in the ballad genre; however, Levering's plays present a sense and site of reconciliation and healing. Members of the community are *still* unable to talk about it as the grief and trauma from their ancestors is passed down to them even over a century later. In remembering this event, emotions run high, but the plays represent an attempt to come together. It is an opportunity for the community to heal by observing a more humanistic, tragic portrayal of the shoot-out, a rhetorical remembering that is reminiscent of the one presented in "Claude Allen." Housed in the historic courthouse, this new remembering, however, resides in the realism of the characters involved and is centered on an attempt to heal the fissure of the town caused by the shoot-out.

Levering's ability to write the play as a community member helped make the play more realistic. Even though he returned from living in Los Angeles, Levering easily plugged back into the locale of Hillsville. He wrote *Thunder in the Hills* (two variations exist of this play), *The Capture of the Allen Men*, and most recently *Sidna Allen's Dream* and the second version *Thunder in the Hills*, which was lengthened from a production that lasted 1½ hours to one that is 3½ hours in length. The longer version was performed during the centennial of the shoot-out. Perhaps one of the most interesting parts of these plays is that not only are they written and (mostly) directed by Levering, but also the performers in the plays were *all* Hillsville community members, and the performances took place in the historic courthouse.[4]

When addressing the centennial performance of *Thunder in the Hills*, Levering notes that he was "Trying to tell a community story, a story that belongs to this whole area."[5] Interestingly, as he introduces the play, he evokes the antebellum South, noting that the play is "sort of like Gone with the Wind in Carroll County, maybe it's too long, by the time you get to the end it's kind of a tragic saga that happened here in Carroll County."[6] While the invocation of the antebellum South is interesting (Confederate flags are found frequently throughout Hillsville), perhaps Levering mentions *Gone With the Wind* here because of the epic nature of the newest rendition of the play. As noted earlier, the play is 3½ hours long and is most certainly episodic, much like Mitchell's novel.

Levering's plays offer ancestors and members of the town the opportunity to gather in the historic courthouse where the shoot-out happened and listen to the story together. The plot of the play starts with the episode around the ear of corn at Garland Allen's church and ends after J. Sidna Allen is pardoned and welcomed home by his wife, Betty Allen. The action of the play includes the fight by the Allen boys in the church, the shoot-out itself, the jailing of Floyd and Claude, the electrocution of both men, and the pardoning of J. Sidna Allen. Wendy S. Hesford's idea of spectacular rhetorics helps explain these moments in the plays where the actors address the audience members directly to consider the trauma that happened in the courtroom during the shoot-out. This communal gathering and then participation in the play act as moments of healing rhetoric because the attendance of audience members from both sides of the shoot-out opens the possibility of sympathy for the other side. *Several* community members have told me that "it helped with the healing" of the town. Levering's status as a community member also helped make the play more realistic. The characters are *not* flat and are truthful to historical depictions instead of stereotyped portrayals from outside the region.

While these moments are important, enacting the plays in the historic courthouse works further to increase the emotional impact of the performances; a space where seven people were killed, a site of historical trauma. Levering deliberately uses the exact space to evoke realism as well as a sense of history. The space is currently not used for legislature, but for memorializing the dead and performing the history that took place there. A brief analysis of the space of the historic courthouse demonstrates the contrast of the outlaw rhetorical remembering as it focuses on the deaths there as opposed to the compassionate portrayals from Levering's plays.

An Analysis of the Historic Courthouse

The courthouse has changed little since the shoot-out happened. It was built by Ira Coutrane in 1873.[7] The town stopped using the courthouse in 1997. When first approaching the building, the treasurer's office, located at the right of the building, houses the Historical Society office and the museum. The clerk of court's old office is immediately above the museum and is currently used for storage. When entering the courthouse, you come up the cement steps from Main Street, and there is a Confederate statue immediately in front. This statue was centered in the middle of Main Street, directly in front of the courthouse, during the time of the shoot-out. In fact, numerous accounts state that Floyd hid behind the statue as he fired back at the clerk of court, Dexter Goad, who was on the steps of the courthouse. When climbing the steps from Main Street, you also notice two green stairways. The ones on the right go up to where Dexter Goad's office was located at the time of the shoot-out. There are still bullet holes located within the steps from the shoot-out. Climbing the steps brings you into a hall that leads to the courtroom.

The space of the courthouse does not look as it did when the shoot-out occurred. The law library located across from the actual courtroom was not installed until much later. The judge's bench and the bailiff's bench are all pushed forward. See Fig. 3.1 for a current picture of the courthouse.

Despite the changes in the layout of the courtroom, there are two important memorials that evoke the outlaw rhetorical remembering.

Historic Courthouse, Hillsville. Photograph by author

On the north wall, a plaque stands in honor of Judge Massie. Ronald W. Hall writes that "a fund raising had been initiated the previous May by the State Bar Association under the leadership of Judge R. Carter Scott."[8] The plaque reads as follows:

> Erected by the state bar association of Virginia as a memorial to the legal accomplishments, the fidelity to duty and the courage unto death of Thornton Lemmon Massie Judge of the Twenty First VA Circuit who was assassinated while holding court in the courthouse of Carroll County Virginia on the Fourteenth of March 1912. To die in the discharge of duty is to live forever in hearts which honor courage and patriotism.

The use of the word *assassinated* is important because it demonstrates that this memorial most certainly deems Massie's murder as the fault of the Allens and perpetuates the outlaw remembering. In its closing statements, the plaque says Massie was serving his country while on the bench. Both statements regard Massie highly and describe his honorable service as a judge and civil servant until he was gunned down by the Allens.

Above the text, there is a Greco-Roman statue of a woman with a large feather in her hand. She has recently placed a wreath on a large door with a lion's head as the door handle. The figure could be the Greco-Roman goddess Athena, since she is holding what could be understood as an owl feather. The owl is often seen with the goddess, which associates her with wisdom and the law. In the memorials of Judge Massie, we often see him referred to as wise or having wisdom. The symbol of the door handle is also important because lions often symbolize bravery.

In addition to Judge Massie's memorial, there is another plaque dedicated to the victims who were killed in the courtroom that also reaffirms the outlaw rhetorical remembering. Ronald W. Hall notes that this plaque was one of two. The other plaque was "dedicated in the courtroom in Wytheville"; however, this "identical plaque" faces from the south wall of the courthouse in Hillsville.[9] The plaque for the victims reads:

> ERECTED BY THE STATE BAR ASSOCIATION OF
> VIRGINIA IN MEMORY OF
> WILLIAM M. FOSTER - COMMONWATHER'S ATT'Y
> LEWIS F. WEBB - SHERIFF
> AUGUSTUS C. FOWLER - MEMBER OF THE JURY
> BETTIE [*sic*] AYERS - A WITNESS IN THE CASE THEN UNDER TRIAL
> WHO WERE ASSASSINATED IN THIS COURTHOUSE
> WHILE IN DISCHARGE OF THEIR DUTY TO THE
> COMMONWEALTH ON THE 14TH OF MARCH 1912

First, naming each victim gives power and significance to each individual. The plaque continues to use the word *assassinated* here because these victims were killed in cold blood in the courthouse (some dying outside, some later the next day). Similar to Judge Massie's plaque, this plaque wants to show that the victims were legislatively bound to this space and were doing their civic duty.

In addition to the text, another shrouded Greco-Roman woman places a wreath on top of a tomb that has "In Memoriam" written on it. Unlike the statue at Judge Massie's memorial, this statue has no identifying features but is just placing another wreath on the grave. This woman is also significant to the Allen women who were left behind to mourn and rebuild their lives after their husbands were killed, executed, or incarcerated. What is also different in this plaque is that it is signed in the bottom right corner. The signature is a circle with a line through it. While this could be a symbol of the Freemasons, whose signage still pervade many structures in Hillsville, including Sidna Allen's Victorian home, this signature is not identifiable.

This thick description is necessary to understanding the juxtaposition of the play to the memorials of the courthouse. The plaques on the wall and the layout of the courthouse both demonstrate that the courthouse *still* stands as a place of memory evoking the Allens as outlaw figures. It still remembers the tragic event that happened there without acknowledging the deaths of the Allen men who died later because of the shoot-out.

Affective Transmissions: A New Way to Approach the Plays

Frank Levering realizes the power of remembrance in the courthouse. He knows how placing the play in the historic courthouse itself will have an impact on the actors, the audience, and the play itself despite how these memorials convey the Allens. He comments on the intertwining of the local actors and the courthouse:

> the actors being so good and the fact that oral tradition of this area, the story that everybody has very strong feelings about

> made this a unique experience I don't think you could have done this in any other play. And to have it here in this courtroom space where the shootout actually took place and then make a theatrical space of this courtroom kind of a space where everybody thinks of a public space, a community space I think was a very important element.[10]

Many of these actors have ancestors who were involved in the shoot-out. Some of the actors even played on the opposite side of their ancestors in the play. Victor Allen, direct descendant of Garland Allen and named after his ancestor, played Sheriff Lewis Webb in the play. He admitted, "I got no qualms with playing Lew. The play has really helped heal the town."[11] His testimonial demonstrates that the play's sympathetic view to both sides of the shoot-out offers a sense of coming together.

Witnessing the play in the historical space places the performance in juxtaposition to the outlaw rhetorical remembering suggested by the memorials on the walls. As Victor Allen stated above, it helps "heal the town" because the play sympathizes with both sides of the shoot-out, rejecting the stereotypical outlaw image. Without seeing it performed in the courthouse, there is a sense of loss in the tension between the outlaw image of the courthouse and the sympathetic, traumatic lens of the play. Levering elaborates on the play's temporary nature, noting that the actors and the location in the courthouse

> made it an extraordinary experience and hard to repeat. You do it and it's gone. Thanks to you [Bill Webb] it won't be gone because it's recorded. Live theatre is a powerful thing and like now it's all over. You have to do it and then let it go. Just let go of it.[12]

Watching the play live in the courthouse adds to the interchange between the outlaw remembering and the tragic narrative remembering that the play portrays. As Denise Taylor asserts "performance [. . .] insists on physical presence: one can participate only by *being there.*"[13] Live theater is exactly that, live. Actors can interact with the audience in ways that are not possible if the play is watched in a private space. There was something missing when I watched the play in my living room on my television instead of in the courtroom. While technology made it available, there was most certainly an absence or an abstention of place. Rebecca Schneider describes how the "mode of access" to the play changed for me: "In the archive, the performance of access is a ritual act that, by occlusion and inclusion, scripts the depreciation of (and registers as disappeared) other modes of access."[14] As I watched the play, I was stripped of the ethereal experience of being in that space and experiencing the tension of those two rememberings. I was on a comfortable couch and could pause the 3½-hour play when I needed to, whereas the audience members sitting on the hard, wooden courthouse benches and observing the play in person could not get up until the intermission unless they wanted to disturb other audience members.

In addition to this loss in experience, pieces of the transmission of the remembering were lost to me as I sat on my couch to watch the play. The memorialization of the courthouse was not evident on the DVD recording; instead, the focus was on the play itself. I lost the outlaw remembering of the courthouse and focused only on the tragic in what Schneider deems the "repeated act of securing memory."[15] She asserts that my loss in not being there is

> to rethink the *site of history in ritual representation.* This is not to say that we have reached the "end of history," neither is it to say that past events didn't happen, nor that to access the past is impossible. It is rather to resituate the site of any *knowing of history as body-to-body transmission.* Whether that ritual representation is the attendance to documents in the library [. . .], or the oral tales of family lineage [. . .], or the myriad traumatic reenactments engaged in both consciously and unconsciously, *we refigure "history" onto bodies, the affective transmissions of showing and telling.*[16]

She notes that the transmission itself is embodied in both actor and audience member (or rhetor and audience), which acts to keep the play alive. Even though it's ephemeral, the shoot-out still exists because it has been acted out and put into the world through the body of the actors. Because performance theory tells us that the ephemeral has value in preserving, affecting, and moving archives, then the ephemeral must have rhetorical value in public memory studies. No matter how it is watched, the experience of watching affects the viewer through the emotional effect of the play itself. For instance, the ephemeral is made into public memory by my watching the play on a DVD miles away from Hillsville and years away from when the play was performed—it is still an enactment, still a performance of that memory. Its materialistic form allows it to be studied despite a certain amount of affect being lost to the viewer.

"You're Greedy for Guns and Blood": Spectacular Moments in the Play

In addition to the presence of the audience in the historic courtroom, there are four particular places in the play that break the fourth wall or that dictate and speak to the presence of the play in the here and now. These moments in the play not only self-identify it as a play but also acknowledge its presence in a historical site—a site that once represented a place of trauma and fissure but now represents coming together, mourning, and healing. In these four places in the play, the characters are cognizant of themselves as characters in a play in the courthouse. They not only engage with the audience but also speak to the moment in time and physicality of where they exist. The opening introduction with Frances Allen, the actual shoot-out in the courthouse, Floyd's and Claude's deaths by electrocution, and the final words by Frances and Floyd Allen are examples of how these performances produce what Taylor calls ghosts who "tap into public fantasies and leave a trace, reproducing and at time altering culture repertoires."[17] The performance itself

> provokes emotions it claims only to represent, evokes memories and grief that belong to some other body. It conjures up and makes visible not just the living but the powerful army of the always already living. The power of seeing through performance is the recognition that we've seen it all before—the fantasies that shape our sense of self, of community, that organize our scenarios of interaction, conflict, and resolution.[18]

These moments re-create Hillsville's traumatic history in a compelling way. They most definitely evoke "memories and grief" and make those feelings tangible. In the play, Floyd's mental anguish while in jail and Frances's agony stand as two of the most powerful instances of how "memories and grief" collide to create a sense of empathetic realism.

To name these performative moments, I borrow from Wendy Hesford's term, *spectacular rhetoric*. According to Hesford, spectacular rhetoric means "to highlight the visual rhetoric of human rights, of which the spectacle is only a part, and to accommodate audiovisual and mixed-media forms and rhetorical techniques [. . .] that are used in speech and writing to convey experiences of vision."[19] Breaking apart from the "human rights" aspect of her definition, these moments in the play do function as spectacle because they reveal the actors not only as objects of the audience's gaze in the play but also as emblems in healing the town. In her words, they indeed "acquire social value and symbolic overtones from larger frames of reference," as they give value to the shoot-out and demonstrate its role in Hillsville.[20] They make a spectacle of the shoot-out, but they do it in a way that blurs the line between past and present, good and bad, and the Allens' side of the shoot-out and the local government's side. These spectacular moments create a sense of catharsis in the play where sympathy for both sides is felt by the audience and the sympathetic, tragic rhetorical remembering occurs. Particular moments by Betty Allen and Frances Allen are especially important in conveying empathy, but I will address those in chapter 5.

Here for Trouble: The First Spectacular Moment

Frances Allen's opening testimony immediately breaks the fourth wall between past and present by addressing the morbid curiosity of the audience, who want to see the event re-created; she is creating a spectacular moment in all senses of the word. Referred to as the "woman in woe" in many news accounts, Frances states, "what do you want from me now [. . .] once ain't enough for you [. . .] greedy for guns and blood [. . .] you want to see folks shot, dead. That's what you're here for, trouble."[21] Through her character, Levering acknowledges people's curiosity and how disturbing it is that they are interested in an event that resulted in the deaths of seven people.[22] Frances is working against the outlaw remembering portrayed in the newspapers. Her voice of reason conveys tragedy and pity for her family. Schneider elaborates on the breaking of the wall between past and present when she writes,

> The past can disrupt the present [. . .], but so too can the present disrupt the past [. . .]; neither are entirely "over" nor discrete, but partially and porously persist. Something is different here than simply remembering, or simple negotiation with "a time gone by."[23]

Frances Allen's opening testimony does indeed "disrupt the present" because she makes the audience consider the cruel nature of revisiting the shoot-out. Her voice reflects the feelings of the many residents who blatantly do *not* want to talk about the shoot-out, both right after it happened and now. In fact, some local community members refer to it as "the incident," "the tragedy," or just "the shoot-out." The event brings up too many bad memories and was simply not something to be discussed. This silence is echoed by Jezebel Goad and Maude Iroler in chapter 5. However, this silence is juxtaposed with

Frances's statement that "once ain't enough for you." Through this statement, she argues that, despite the silence around it, the shoot-out is always there; the tragedy cannot be undone.

Frances Allen's testimony ends by transitioning to an explanation of how the shoot-out started in Garland Allen's church and how that small event led to the deaths of those in the courthouse. She states, "If you's ever at a corn shuckin' [. . .] you turn your head away and make a beeline for that door [. . .] seven people died before their time and the rest of them died still feeling the chilly prickles of what they seen here."[24] This invocation of the courtroom deems the space as a place of death, destruction, and trauma to those who witnessed it. Ending her opening testimony and moving into Floyd's initial speech, Frances states how we, as the audience, have the right to decide which side we are on "'Cause *you* are the jury."[25] This invocation for the audience to decide is similar to the duty of the jury at the actual trial to morally act for or against the Allens. Again, here we see a convergence of past and present merging in Frances Allen's call for action, with the audience asked to consider the case anew and to engage with it rather than ignore it.

Ghosts of the Past and Present: The Second Spectacular Moment

The second spectacular moment in the play is before the actual shoot-out. Levering draws attention to the fact that Floyd and Claude were not with Frances the night before the shoot-out. The night was stormy, and the play depicts Frances as frantic. She talks in third person about the storm, herself, and the impending death: "[Wind] and rain like Noah's flood arising. What could Frances Allen do? Old before her time because it's gone back so fast. Death coming quick."[26] With this scene, Levering sets up Frances Allen as a figure who truly suffered before and after the shoot-out. Her character is built in moments of emotional turmoil. In the play, she develops as a character, whereas in most of the male-dominated newspaper accounts, she is largely absent. Her character is figuratively and literally haunted by the shoot-out as two shoot-out victims appear to her. The trauma she suffers is real and contributes to the sympathetic, traumatic rhetorical remembering in this depiction.

Betty Ayers, a witness who was shot in the courtroom but died outside the courthouse, appears to Frances asking, "What was you going to do with the rest of your life?" to which Frances replies "I have lost myself and there is no place for me deep down."[27] Through this exchange, Frances's grief and loss of self is truly expressed. The deaths of Floyd, and Claude in particular, have left her a childless widow. Furthermore, Betty's ghost represents not only a character but also a ghost who, as Diana Taylor notes, "continues to act politically even as it exceeds the live."[28] She is one of two ghosts who haunt both Frances in the play and the audience in their remembrance of the shoot-out and the death suffered in that very space. Like the plaques that adorn the walls of the courthouse, her appearance is a physical representation of those who died there.

Next, Augustus Fowler visits Frances. Like Betty, who claims she died outside, Augustus points to the very spot where he died in the courtroom. This performance again represents a clash of the past and present. Merely feet from where they sit watching this performance, the audience becomes aware of when and where his death took place. Augustus then states, "I got nothing against Floyd that we can't settle our accounts down yonder," to which Frances replies, "I ain't got no family [. . .] you leave this earth. You go farm in hell."[29] Instead of the pity expressed by Betty and Frances, this is rather a brash exchange that most certainly represents the lingering resentment the town feels for the Allen family. Frances does, however, stand up for herself and does not cower from Augustus's ghost. After this exchange, Frances then yells, "Where are the rest of you? Why won't you speak to me?"[30] Her demands for response are eerie enough to read, but hearing them in the actual courthouse makes them even more unnerving.

Her calling to the ghosts of the victims represents a penance of her character to those who were killed for her husband's trial. In addition, this action represents something much bigger. It represents the silence that has overshadowed the town since the shoot-out. Not only did Betty Allen (Sidna's wife) and Frances Allen become outcasts in the town, but the shoot-out itself was not talked about. The trauma was too much for those who were involved. Frances's invocation of the spirits represents a call for conversation among the past residents of Hillsville, as well as those in the present. It is through conversation and scenes like this one in the play that the strife and trauma that each person went through during the shoot-out are articulated. The invocation creates a sympathetic rhetorical remembering that describes the real interactions between those involved in the shoot-out and not the exploited actions created by the media. By having local actors (and family members of those involved) act in the plays while performing them in the *actual* courtroom, conversation *has* to happen about the shoot-out; the outlaw and uncivilized other rememberings are no longer useful. From these conversations come the sense of healing that several residents said happened after the plays were performed. These performances bridged the gap between past and present—they unearthed the trauma and bitterness and brought it out in the open to be discussed. The play does not avoid the three most emotional events related to the shoot-out: the shoot-out itself, the electrocutions of Floyd and Claude, and the final words of Frances and Floyd.

The Shoot-Out on the Stage: The Third Spectacular Moment

Levering's portrayal of the shoot-out is realistic and tasteful. The traumatic event is reenacted with gunshots, which is shocking, but it memorializes the tragedy in a way that provokes emotion from both sides. First, J. Sidna Allen comes out and talks about how he'll never forget what happened in the courtroom. He also talks about the circulation in and around the shoot-out:

> All them years in the State pen in Richmond. Not a day went by that I didn't think about what happened here. What did happen here, there have been so many tales and outright lies told. It has been hard to see through the smoke to see the truth. Now memory, memory is like a loaded pistol it can turn agin' who's holdin' it. Now, somedays I can remember clear as creek water.[31]

J. Sidna Allen's remarks mention his pensive time spent in the penitentiary in Richmond, as well as the circulation of the shoot-out. As mentioned in chapter 1, he knew about the "tales and outright lies" that the media printed about the shoot-out. These comments illustrate the penance of his character, but perhaps what is most interesting here is Levering's use of memory. He, not surprisingly, connects memory with truth that is surrounded by smoke from a loaded pistol. While this metaphor could be regarded as trite and a little too simplistic, it's necessary because it demonstrates how memory is *not* finite and that there are, as J. Sidna Allen remarked in his memoir, "many truths." It resonates with the audience, who understands the connection between memory and the gun violence that happened in the courthouse. The concept that the gun can "turn agin' who's holdin' it" represents how memory is *not* stable. It changes over time, even if a person who was present at the event is the teller of the tale. The changing memories affected not only the oral re-creation of the event but also had legal stature in the pardoning trials of J. Sidna Allen, Wesley Edwards, Sidna Edwards, and many other Allen men.

After J. Sidna Allen's comments, we hear from Alverta Edwards, the mother of Wesley and Sidna (the boys who got in a fight in Garland Allen's church). She states, "This room was standing room only. You know if you were anywhere else you wouldn't be anywhere else.

There were babies in here. God help them for what was coming their way."[32] These comments validate how popular Floyd Allen's trial was at the time. Most citizens of Hillsville (and the surrounding counties) were at the trial because it was entertaining to them. These statements point to not only the popularity of the trial but also to the innocents who were in the courtroom that day. The mention of babies to signify innocence is basic; however, when thinking about the death of young Betty Ayers, who was merely a witness, it's accurate.

After Alverta's plea for the innocent we, again, hear from J. Sidna Allen, but we also hear from Dexter Goad, the county clerk, who Levering portrays as having political and personal strife against the Allens. J. Sidna Allen remarks that "Deck [Dexter] Goad has his eye on me. No doubt in my mind that he would kill me if he could get away with it [. . .] kill me and Floyd both." Goad replies, "Twenty minutes go by. Whatever happens I am here to enforce the law. I have no reason to kill anyone. A man has to keep his chin up. His courage up. To show no sign of weakness."[33] This exchange demonstrates the tension between the Allens and Goad. Levering, at this point in the play, portrays Goad as defensive by wanting Judge Massie to carry a gun to court and practicing shooting the morning of the shoot-out. Massie states that he will not be bullied by the Allens to carry a gun into his own courtroom. The exchange between J. Sidna Allen and Dexter Goad also creates tension in the play and in the room as a whole.

The next spectacular moment during the shoot-out happens immediately after Judge Massie dies and says that "Sid" Allen was the man who shot him. All the victims are lying on the floor, and the Allen men have left the scene. Frances Allen, again, becomes the mediator between the past and the present, the dead and the living, the Allens and the local government. She walks out and says, "There weren't no sun that day. Four days after Lewis Webb died, Nancy died."[34] She notes that Augustus Fowler comes to see her. Lew Foster hasn't come to see her yet, and that they "Took Massie back to Pulaski on the train."[35] When she mentions each dead character's name, he or she leaves the scene of the crime. It's a surreal moment in the play because each of them gets up literally where each victim was shot and moves off stage. The memory of each of these characters is embodied by each actor and remembered separately as they exit the performing area. Unlike the names that merely adorn the memorials on the wall, the exit of each character acknowledges the tragic loss of each of their lives.

Frances Allen concludes the scene with another acknowledgement of the audience and their morbid curiosity. Her voice grows louder as she states, "And I wish you had not thought to come here and acted like it was something you needed to see. Claude, Floyd, all the rest of them didn't have [indiscernible] All of you right here are watching."[36] These comments, again, acknowledge the space and the trauma that occurred there. In this instance, she shames the audience for their morbid curiosity. Her mentioning of Claude and Floyd also illustrates that they didn't have a chance. She, like the audience that observes the play, could not take any sort of action in what went on in the shoot-out.

"Put to Death by the State of Virginia": The Electrocutions of Floyd and Claude

Besides the actual shoot-out, the electrocutions of Floyd and Claude are the second most powerful scenes in the play that include spectacular moments where the past and present collide, the space of the courtroom is acknowledged, and the tragic rhetorical remembering is engaged. The scene builds with Floyd's emotional breakdown in his jail cell, which is constructed from metal pipes. He asks forgiveness of his wife and God, saying, "The Lord says blessed is those who mourn,

I am not blessed."[37] This depiction of Floyd follows the same transformation of his character in the media from violent hillbilly to convicted, empathetic prisoner. Like his wife, Frances, Floyd has his own fictional visit, specifically of Dexter Goad visiting him in his jail cell. Floyd states, "Deck Goad with your pistol drawn." Goad replies, "No one ever forgets us in this courtroom. We are two sworn enemies who draw our guns in the theatre of another man's mind. Hell bent, Hell bent on destroying the lives, fortunes, of Dexter Goads or Floyd Allens. Floyd, I trust you made peace with God."[38] The actual historical documentation of this visit is insignificant to this part in the play; Goad more than likely did not visit Floyd in jail since they were "sworn enemies." However, this visit represents a peace offering from Goad that may not have existed in reality. It demonstrates not only the memory of the shoot-out, but also a fictional olive branch between the political factions involved.

The "[drawing of guns] in the theatre of another man's mind" works in two ways. The first is what J. Sidna Allen referred to earlier in his remembering of the incident. The impartiality of memory of the incident, that is, collective memory and the retelling of the event, brings about many different variations of the memory. The second is the literal play that is happening in the minds of the audience who is watching it. They're creating their own beliefs about not only the characters in the play but also the actual people on whom Levering bases the play. Despite either interpretation of the line, both of them destroy the lives and fortunes of Goad and Floyd Allen. This statement in the play is a bit of an embellishment, as Dexter Goad remained in Hillsville and lived a successful life working in the courthouse, whereas Floyd's family was splintered and utterly traumatized after the shoot-out. Only recently are family members willing to speak out about "the incident." The lines do acknowledge the destruction of the shoot-out and attempt to resolve the conflict between Floyd Allen and Dexter Goad regardless of whether it actually happened.

Frances's Last Words: The Final Spectacular Moment

The final cry of Frances and final words of Floyd in the last scene establish the final spectacular moment that depicts the tragic rhetorical remembering. In the scene, Frances again comments on the courtroom, saying, "This place here where I never come and never will again."[39] It is a symbolic and literal gesture that she will no longer go back to the courtroom because of the trauma that she suffered there. She then moves her commentary to the funeral of Floyd and Claude, where Claude's coffin was open and where there was the "awfullest crowd you ever laid eyes on."[40] Her description of the funeral displays her hatred of Floyd for causing the trouble: "[I] walked past Floyd and I never did, would not look at my husband. When I came to Claude, I cradled my boy. I cradled him in my arms. I cradled my cold baby. He was so cold for the longest time."[41] Clearly, we see her disgust for Floyd. The scene matches eyewitness accounts from people who noticed Frances not looking at her husband and holding her son at the actual funeral. Her actions show how traumatic this event was for her. The emotion in the scene is palpable.

After the funeral, she turns back to address the audience one last time to combine both present and past. She says,

> Hear that March wind a-blowin'? Well you all had to come see this again, a-lookin' at us this way. All the things we've done tried to do and tried not to do. So now you all go home tonight, crawl into your beds and have yourself a sweet dream. I hope you all are well satisfied.[42]

The initial weather reference puts us back at the month of the shoot-out, but more importantly, she addresses the audience for the final time. She references not only the play but also the audience's perception of the shoot-out through the play as she notes "[all] the things we've done tried to do and tried not to do." This comment also references the *many* depictions of the shoot-out that demonize either the

Allen family or the local government. Her final words reach beyond the scope of the play to the audience. Through Frances, Levering attempts to convey the temporality of the play while also expressing how the performance will stay with the audience. At the end of the play, the audience is "well satisfied" but is left to ponder why they desire to see more of the violence and trauma of the incident. They *want* to witness the spectacle of the shoot-out. These final remarks by Frances make the play personal for each member of the audience, expanding its impact beyond the walls of the courthouse. She breaks down their initial perceptions of the play and their desire to see the violence and trauma enacted. Frances's dialogue here reinforces the transition of the shoot-out from trauma to spectacle in the eyes of the viewers.

While this final reflective moment seems like a good ending to the play, Levering then has Floyd come out at the very end and yell, "Gentlemen, gentlemen, I ain't a-goin'." In the performance in 2012, the audience laughs at this line because it seems rather comedic after the seriousness of Frances's lines beforehand. Floyd's dialogue undoes all the emotional reflection that Frances set up earlier; the line draws the audience back to the violent mountaineer rhetorical remembering instead of the tragic, sympathetic one that Frances's final speech represents. The audience reckons with their desire to see the violence of the play, and then Floyd comes out and bellows his famous line. Levering wants to include Floyd here to demonstrate the key moment of the trial, but it falls flat to a moment of comedy. Despite its comedic tone, the line still resonates and echoes in the memory of the courthouse and of those who watch the play. It demonstrates that Floyd is bound to the memory of Hillsville and the shoot-out. It is after Floyd said this that seven people died and the lives of everyone in the courthouse and the town of Hillsville were changed.

Close readings of these scenes where past and present collide affirm Rebecca Schneider's view that the play has staying power beyond the courthouse. While Levering and many other performance scholars state that the performance is temporary, its embodiment in the local gives it staying power. Even Frances Allen in the last scene notes that the audience will think about the play as they "crawl into [their] beds and have [. . .] a safe dream." Embodiment does not stay only on the stage though; as mentioned earlier, I would argue that it is the coming together of the descendants of the shoot-out in the courthouse that brings power and healing to the space. The traumatic, spectacular incident deemed unspeakable by those who witnessed it is now enacted and embraced by those buying tickets to see it. These moments enable the tragic rhetorical remembering to not only exist but also to juxtapose the outlaw rhetorical rememberings of the memorials on the courthouse walls. Both the actors and the audience "refigure 'history' onto [their] bodies, the affective transmissions of showing and telling."[43] The commodification of the event renders it a spectacle, but because of the emotions behind the play, the performance serves as a site of healing. By the end, both the actors and the audience are indeed "well satisfied" as they acknowledge what happened in the past and how that past affects the present conditions of their own lives as they continue to heal from the tragedy.

The Disruptive Past: How the Ballads and Plays Perform in the Present

Chapters 2 and 3 explore how the ballads and the plays combine memory and performance theory to produce a new rhetorical remembering that portrays trauma, pity, and sympathy for those involved in the shoot-out. The plays work as what performance theorists call archives—they retain a historical memory of the shoot-out. That memory is reconstructed in the performance of the play. On the other hand, the ballads illustrate the fissure in Hillsville with images of a violent J. Sidna Allen and a sympathetic, pitiful Claude Allen. These ballads mirror the uptake of two of the rememberings mentioned in chapter 1. One ballad creates the violent hillbilly gangster rememberings, and the other ballad conveys sympathy and tragedy. Decades later, Levering's plays continue the tragic lens that the "Claude Allen" ballad uses. The performances counter the violent memory of the courthouse as a place of murder and convert the courthouse to a place where people can heal from the trauma of the shoot-out. The plays take out the stereotypes that the ballads reinforce and replaces them with fact (albeit the plays could be deemed historical fiction).

Despite how the ballads and plays fissure or heal the feelings in the town, both types of performance produce emotions and memories about the historical event. Returning to the ideas of Diana Taylor, we notice that these performances are powerful. Either type "evokes memories and grief that belong to some other body. It conjures up and makes visible not just the living but the powerful army of the always already living."[44] These "memories and grief" belong to the bodies that are represented by the singers or actors, and they belong to the still-traumatized citizens of the town in which they are performed. The act of seeing the performance changes those who see it: "the fantasies that shape our sense of self, of community, that organize our scenarios of interaction, conflict, and resolution."[45] The ideas of conflict and resolution are relevant here because historically the recent plays demonstrate that the community of Hillsville is ready to heal from the event, whereas the "Sidna Allen" ballad split the town. The plays reject the rhetorical remembering of the media stereotypes and embrace a remembering of the shoot-out based on reality, trauma, and pity.

These portrayals of the shoot-out demonstrate how it continues to be memorialized as seen in the performances of the plays during the shoot-out's Centennial Symposium (*not* celebration). Those who attended the plays were welcome to visit the grave sites of the victims of the shoot-out, including Floyd and Claude Allen. Similar to the courthouse during the play, the invocation and visitation of these sites demonstrates a change in the town's feelings toward the shoot-out. Both the Allen side and the local government side were sympathetic to each other. The memories themselves are not being re-created, but rather the stances felt by the ancestors and people of Hillsville have changed. The days of regarding the shoot-out as a grudge are passing. The movement from the fissure of the media, the "Sidna Allen" ballad, and the violence of the historical courthouse memorials to the emotional, healing, empathetic portrayals of the plays changes the effect and circulation of the shoot-out today.

"Feelings Are Still Very Strong"

Sites of Public Memory in Hillsville, Virginia

> Gunfire, chaos, and death ensued [. . .] All in a moment.
>
> Exhibit in the Carroll County Historical Society and Museum

I arrived at the historic J. Sidna Allen House as rain started to fall from the sky much like the day of the trial; however, it's a warm day in July 2016 instead of a frosty morning in March 1912. The weather was appropriate to set the mood about the house whose first residents only lived there for six months. As I walked up, people ran to their cars to avoid the rain. There had just been a media event there to discuss fundraising from the plays to pay for renovations for the house.[1] Women gathered up easels as I walked up the porch steps—the porch where decades earlier Floyd and J. Sidna Allen might have stood to weigh their options for Floyd's trial the next day. The porch itself seemed stable, unlike the warped flooring inside the house I would explore later; however, the white paint was peeling all over the outside of the house. While in the dining room, I met Stu Shenk, who played J. Sidna Allen in Levering's plays. He began to tell me and another visiting couple the story of the shoot-out. I realized that he, too, performed the story as he told it just as the actors in the play, concentrating on the male-centered violence.

Shenk's oral storytelling is not the only way the shoot-out is remembered, but it is also preserved in the personal archives of local Hillsville residents that keep artifacts from and about the shoot-out in their own homes. Much like the media, ballads, and plays mentioned in earlier chapters, these personal archives often still participate in the outlaw and tragic rhetorical rememberings invoking masculine, or male-centered, violence, but in a way that depends on the orality and passing down of the event. These retellings are not official, but rather depend on unofficial, independent ways of retelling depending on the speaker.

Gary Marshall, local native of Hillsville, has over fifteen file boxes of memorabilia associated with the shoot-out. These boxes contain newspaper clippings, copies of a rock opera based on the shoot-out, and items from the Centennial Symposium, among other things. Another informant found the original verdict that was handed to Judge Massie right before the shots were fired. He calls it the "Holy Grail" of the shoot-out. And yet another person emailed me various pictures of the medal that was cast by a local women's group for Claude Allen after his death. These examples clearly demonstrate that residents in Hillsville want to re-create their own vernacular histories of the event. John Bodnar, in *Remaking America: Public Memory, Commemoration, and Patriotism in the Twentieth Century*, notes that these vernacular histories "convey what social reality feels like rather than what it should be like. Its very existence threatens the sacred and timeless nature of official expressions."[2] The citizens of Hillsville collect these not only for personal nostalgia but also so they can retell the story in their own way. These small personal collections do not stand as government-sanctioned or official histories of the event. Rather, they show how the residents want to reclaim the narrative and create their own version of the shoot-out, one that is wound up in artifact and almost always rooted in the story passed down from their ancestors in Hillsville. With each artifact from their small archives, their voice lends itself to a particular kind of remembering of the event. In addition to these vernacular histories, there are three museums near Hillsville that remember the shoot-out in vernacular and official ways.

These vernacular and official rhetorical rememberings develop from the stories created by each museum and rely on epideictic rhetoric to tell these stories. Epideictic rhetoric develops from the conduct and values of the society that constructs the piece of rhetoric. Innately, the piece of rhetoric is tied to the vernacular histories of that society as they construct these values from their own interactions with each other. The retelling of a historical event becomes rhetorical as it interweaves the historical and personal aspects of the history. It contains the actual action of the historical event as well as the individual or the public's collective memory of that event. Through these vernacular histories, an official history develops that is generally couched in a public sphere, i.e., a place of public memory or remembrance. These places support the following argument by Cynthia Miecznkowski Sheard:

> Epideictic discourse today operates in contexts civic, professional or occupational, pedagogical, and so on that invite individuals to evaluate the communities or institutions to which they belong, their own roles within them, and the roles and responsibilities of their fellow constituents, including their leaders.[3]

Generally, museums display their own versions of *how* the society remembers the historical event, as Sheard mentioned above. Each museum retells the story in different ways, some relying on official retellings that are sanctioned by an aspect of government or an organization, while some can be more vernacular in nature, relying on the artifacts and the museum curators to construct the rhetorical remembering of the event. Each version reveals what the curator or collector of the museum deems valuable in the retelling of the shoot-out.

The Carroll County Historical Society and Museum presents visitors with a view of the shoot-out that includes the reformed craftsman J. Sidna Allen as well as vernacular histories contained on a peg board in the museum. This mostly vernacular exhibit presents a humanized rhetorical remembering by showing that the Allens were responsible citizens in Hillsville. The Mount Airy Museum of Regional History, a government-sanctioned museum, offers an overview of the shoot-out that includes the capture and final trial of the Allen men. The details of the shoot-out are tacked to a piece of carpet spanning only one short wall of the three-floor museum. This remembering humanizes both sides of the shoot-out, but it also sensationalizes the event by following newspaper depictions of it. Lastly, the Harmon Museum, located in the back of a western wear and boots store, gives us a purely vernacular take on the shoot-out that includes a one-sided view of the Baldwin–Felts Detective Agency. The story it conveys is historical but also personal. Each newspaper clipping is accompanied by an artifact, such as pictures taken of the shoot-out, family photographs, and Floyd Allen's saddlebags. These rhetorical rememberings from chapter 1 and each of these sites of public memory create a new way of retelling the story of the shoot-out.

Epideictic History Making through Vernacular and Official Stories

These sites of public memory, using differing rhetorical rememberings, entail many variations of the shoot-out that engage the vernacular history of the region but also attempt to make the history official by placing it in an exhibit, whether that be under glass or merely thumbtacked to a poster. These vernacular retellings give rise to epideictic history making of the shoot-out. Each of these museums encourages a shared history of the courthouse shoot-out. They are all within an hour drive of each other. The Harmon Museum and Carroll County Historical Society and Museum are only minutes apart. The Mount Airy Museum of Regional History is thirty minutes away. However, they do not share exhibits. The stories are kept separate at each museum, and materials are not exchanged. They each retain their own rhetorical remembering of the shoot-out.

Each museum offers different ways to approach their exhibits about Hillsville. Dickinson, Blair, and Ott state, "the primary action the rhetoric of the memory place invites is the performance of traveling to and traversing it. That effort to participate in a memory place's rhetoric almost certainly predisposes its visitors to respond in certain ways."[4] Each of these museums continues to participate in epideictic retellings as materials combine to tell their version of the story about the shoot-out. The way the curators set up each exhibit guides patrons to view the shoot-out in particular ways.

While knowledge of the region is relevant, artifacts also help patrons construct or evaluate the community of Hillsville. Sometimes the traversing of the museum goes opposite as in the Carroll County Historical Society and Museum, which starts with the furniture that J. Sidna Allen made during his incarceration in Richmond. After this large exhibit, visitors see a carving that depicts those involved in the shoot-out, a medal given to Jezebel Goad, and then a peg board that explains the shoot-out. This is different from the exhibit at the Mount Airy Museum of Regional History, which explicitly takes readers chronologically through each step of the shoot-out and includes a brief regional commentary on Hillsville itself at the beginning. These rhetorical choices provide visitors with ways of approaching the shoot-out that rhetorically builds its history. By beginning with J. Sidna Allen's furniture, the Carroll County Historical Society and Museum presents a reformed depiction of the Allen men. By introducing the town and then going into the shoot-out, the Mount Airy Museum of Regional History guides visitors through a linear path to tell the story of the event. In fact, they include "story" in much of the materials in their exhibits and within their own development as a museum.

While traveling through the three museums, visitors will negotiate their own knowledge of the region with the knowledge that each exhibit conveys. These negotiations can be seen in the Mount Airy Museum of Regional History. The museum presents the Allens as part of Hillsville, but it also portrays them as bootleggers. Patrons can easily attach the drunken hillbilly image to this depiction, although more educated visitors may understand that moonshining was a part of the socioeconomic class at that time in Hillsville and in the Appalachian region generally. In another example, as mentioned above, the exhibit in the Carroll County Historical Society and Museum starts with the woodwork of J. Sidna Allen and ends with a description of the courthouse. Also, similar to the Mount Airy Regional Museum, the Harmon Museum offers a linear path for patrons to follow, with newspaper clippings organized in chronological order. In addition, framed pictures often accompany the newspaper clippings. These artifacts "prescribe particular paths of entry, traversal, and exit. Maps, arrows, walls, boundaries, openings, doors, build of memorial places often function as 'strategy' in Michel de Certeau's sense of the word."[5] While the Harmon Museum does not have a government-hired curator like the others, the ways that these artifacts are placed still rhetorically tells the story that is sanctioned by the museum. An analysis of each of these officially vernacular spaces demonstrates how they each ask viewers to participate in the creation of the history of the shoot-out.

The Museums

"All in a Moment": The Carroll County Historical Society and Museum

Before ascending the green stairs (which have bullet holes in them) to go to the actual historic courtroom, patrons of the Carroll County Historical Society and Museum are encouraged to visit what was once the clerk of court's office. It now serves as the main museum entrance.

When first entering, patrons go through a gift shop and welcome center. There is a welcome table there as well as bookshelves that are lined with local lore about the shoot-out and Hillsville in general. Some of these materials are about the shoot-out, while others are genealogies of the area. In the next room, patrons pass exhibits showing arrowheads and information about coal mining, and then they see the shoot-out exhibit. During the tour, they see the wooden artistry of J. Sidna Allen, hear a brief mention of Jezebel Goad's fictional intervention in the shoot-out, and (in 2016) learn the story as depicted on the peg board, which traces the chronology of the shoot-out. I include the peg board in this analysis because it gives a good background on how the museum rhetorically told the story of the shoot-out during the performance of the Levering plays.

What makes this museum distinct is the guidance of Bill Webb, the curator of the museum. Webb tells the story of the shoot-out as patrons walk through the exhibit. His knowledge of the shoot-out and the exhibit add to the experience as he talks through each artifact. His vernacular storytelling about different pieces reflects an epideictic retelling of the shoot-out as he talks about the community and its role in the shoot-out. For example, he explains where J. Sidna Allen's house is in relation to the museum and promotes recent additions to the exhibits. He praises these pieces that were constructed in the past but demonstrates how they play a role in the present of the museum. His storytelling in the museum humanizes the men and women who were involved. Similar to the audience for the plays, patrons get a sympathetic view of the people in the shoot-out rather than an outlaw rhetorical remembering.

By shaping the rhetorical remembering of the shoot-out in these ways, curators memorialize Floyd's and Claude's deaths and participate in the folklore around the story. Two pieces that are particularly important in this retelling—besides the peg board recounting the shoot-out—are J. Sidna Allen's woodwork and the wooden replica of the shoot-out. Both of these pieces recount a *masculine* retelling of the story since they solely depend on J. Sidna Allen and not his wife or daughters. This remembering is housed in violence but also reformation. Because of his good behavior in jail and his excellent relationship with the guards, J. Sidna Allen was able to establish himself as a well-known carpenter and artist. Upon his release, he traveled the South, displaying and selling his pieces. Many are on loan from his great-grandson, a lawyer in the area. They are extremely valuable, which is why they still remain behind glass. Specifically, two crafted boxes are behind glass. The Mount Airy Museum of Regional History has two similar boxes made by Wesley Edwards, J. Sidna Allen's nephew who fled with him out West. These artifacts reclaim J. Sidna Allen's identity. His reputation in the media as a gangster and violent mountaineer are revoked; instead, he is revered as an artist whose work signifies a reformed member of the judicial system. He no longer stands as the hillbilly outlaw presented in the media and ballads but is now an Appalachian folk artist. Using a particular set of Appalachian and romantic stereotypes to debunk the hillbilly stereotype, J. Sidna Allen is rehumanized.

Next to the large display case, there is a table made in the style of his craftsmanship. Above the table is a piece of paper[6] explaining that it was one of his early works. Interestingly, above the explanation there is a framed picture of Judge Massie, High Sheriff Lewis Webb, and District Attorney William Foster. Much like the plaques in the courthouse, this framed picture stands as a memorial to these men, who died in service of the law. The small memorial falls in between J. Sidna Allen's redemptive woodwork and the wooden carving of the shoot-out itself. Whether intentional or not, this placement of the framed picture represents an interruption in J. Sidna Allen's redemption and a call back to the lives that were lost during the shoot-out. It's also worth noting that these three men are the only ones who occupy the frame. Their civic duty makes them worth remembering, just as the plaques in the courthouse are dedicated to those who were carrying out their civic duty in the courthouse that day. The memory created here is masculine and evokes the consequences of the violence of the shoot-out.

Next to the framed picture is a collage of the shoot-out that characterizes the Allen men as successful businessmen in the region and not violent mountaineers. When I visited the museum in 2016, there was peg board on the opposite wall that displayed an exhibit that the Historical Society had put up to promote the Levering plays taking places in the historic courtroom upstairs. The peg board exhibit echoed the rhetoric of this small collage. The first panel in the collage includes the following caption: "The Allens Prospered—they were a rugged, hardworking family that knew how to make money. Both Floyd and Sidna farmed and owned stores." There is a picture of J. Sidna Allen's store to the left of the caption. These rememberings describe them as working men who provided for their families. This retelling does *not* evoke violence or betrayal, but instead shows that they were productive members of society.

To the right of this explanation, there is a picture of the J. Sidna Allen House. There are also other common pictures of the Allen men from the search and capture of them immediately after the shoot-out. In the middle of the pictures and captions, there is a brief explanation of the shoot-out, complete with a picture of Ronald W. Hall's book, *The Carroll County Courthouse Tragedy*. While this is a marketing ploy to promote the book (and why shouldn't it be since the author is local to the region), the collage still provides an excellent, quick overview of the shoot-out for visitors who are not familiar with its history. This information was repeated on the opposite wall in 2016 on the peg board, and both exhibits tell patrons the basics of the shoot-out. They provide a local depiction that humanizes these individuals. To further push the tragic nature of the shoot-out, the temporary grave marker of Floyd and Claude Allen occurs in both places. The repetition of the marker and its inscription is evidence of how much the museum values this memorial and the local folklore that surrounds it.[7] As mentioned in chapter 1, the marker disappeared after threats from the governor, but according to an Allen family informant, it "is still being used" and is "still in the family." Most of these pictures, including the gravestone, were printed in the local press.

In addition to the pictures and captions, visitors can look down and see a complete wooden carving that re-creates the moment of the shoot-out. Like the play reenactment that I addressed in chapter 2, this re-creation of the shoot-out contains all of the main actors except for the women. The carving was made by a Floyd County resident and housed in a lawyer's office before moving to the museum.[8] Alongside J. Sidna Allen's woodwork, this piece of craftsmanship presents the shoot-out as something distinctly folksy. Each face displays emotion down to Floyd's scowl. We move from J. Sidna Allen's reformation in the previous display to the action of the shoot-out in this model. The model is significant because it presents the shoot-out in a specifically Appalachian folk art tradition, humanizing those involved. It does not present the men as outlaws but merely as the people who were there during the tragedy.

While these depictions are masculine, the Carroll County Historical Society and Museum has the *only* depiction of the women in the shoot-out in a glass case that houses a medal that was cast for Jezebel Goad, Dexter Goad's daughter, by the wife of the governor of Virginia. As noted in chapter 1, there were news reports that Jezebel helped her father reload his gun at the top of the stairs. The museum even has the letter that Governor Mann sent to Jezebel on March 18, 1912.

The letter reflects the same rhetoric that we see in the memorials on the courthouse wall. Jezebel is praised as "a young lady of whom the State of Virginia is, and ought to be proud" for her alleged actions in helping her father defend the courthouse. Immediately, Governor Mann has already gendered her as a "young lady" whom the state should be proud of. The letter continues, offering a deeper glimpse of how gender is constructed. He writes,

> We have the right to expect bravery from our men, but it is rare for a young lady, under such trying circumstances, to exhibit such devotion and heroism. I am very proud of you and know that the people of the county, which produces such men as your father and such daughters as yourself, can be relied on too, to vindicate the law. I have confidence in the good people of Carroll and the highest respect and regards for yourself.

Jezebel's ability to "vindicate the law" sounds awfully familiar. It hearkens back to the declarative statements on the walls of the courthouse (even though those plaques were not posted till years later). Ironically, the last statement in Governor Mann's letter tells Jezebel that he has the "highest respect and regards for yourself." This is ironic for two reasons. First, Governor Mann is completely ignorant of Jezebel's first name, and second, this letter responds to a completely fabricated newspaper article about the shoot-out that reporters created for dramatic effect. Also, right above the medal is a framed picture of her father with his law degree, which steals attention away from Jezebel. However, the inclusion of this medal and the exhibit on Jezebel *does* prove that, even though it is fictional, women do play a part in the epideictic history making in the courthouse museum. Including Jezebel encourages patrons to remember that women were involved during and after the shoot-out. Even though her story is fictionalized, her voice should still be heard. In the next chapter, I give a deeper feminist glimpse into the use of the letter and Jezebel's personal reaction to *not* sharing her information about the shoot-out.

The final part of the shoot-out exhibit was the peg board across the room that contained the story of the shoot-out. It was displayed there in 2016 and has since moved to one of the rooms upstairs in the historic courthouse. This peg board is vernacular because it expects patrons to be able to decipher the story of the shoot-out. In the middle of the peg board, there is a poster that contains the story of the shoot-out; however, this story tends to lean toward the Allen point of view. To the right of the peg board, the words "Social Prejudice," "Political Enmity," "Economic Jealousy," and "Personal Animosity" appear in red. Because of the red font, visitors' eyes are drawn to those words first and then work their way around. Underneath the red words, the phrases "Threats Recorded" and "Inadequate Courtroom Security" appear. Then the right side of the poster says, "December 1910 Nephews and Advisories fight outside Church," "Nephews Indicted; Arrested in N.C.," "Mr. Floyd Allen Intervenes; Charged With Assaulting an Officer," "Mr. Allen on Trial Before a Jury," "Warnings Ignored." These words attempt to retell the events leading up to the shoot-out, focusing on humanizing Floyd's story instead of stereotyping him as an outlaw. While the mention of the nephews tells why, the phrase "Warnings Ignored" alludes to the fact that Judge Massie ignored the warnings that he was supposedly given (and were told to him by other court officials). The display suggests that if Judge Massie had carried a gun or paid attention to the warnings, the shoot-out could have been averted.

In addition, the middle panel continues to lean heavier on the Allen side. It states, "It was a moment on March 14, 1912. Mr. Floyd Allen, then a free citizen, stood to hear the verdict of his peers, upon conviction of inferring with an officer of the law, the jury impose '[*sic*] a sentence of one-year imprisonment." The description "free citizen" is a reminder that Floyd did not have a criminal record prior to the events of the shoot-out. The use of "Mr." shows respect for Floyd, which he did not often receive in the news media. Thus, Floyd is portrayed as a responsible community member and not a criminal. The reference to his sentence of "one-year imprisonment" indicates he was tried and convicted, and this leads to the moment of the actual shoot-out.

The next few descriptions contain the setup of the shoot-out. The first one merely tells about the appeal: "The defense attorney moved for an appeal; Judge Massie agreed to hear the appeal the next morning." The second one emphasizes Floyd's changed status from a free man to a prisoner: "A moment before, Mr. Allen had been a free man; a moment later, a prisoner awaiting appeal. The change was momentous; one which the Allen family was not prepared to accommodate." In other words, they were not ready for violence if the sentence was carried out. Next, the famous words are written: "Mr. Allen is reported to have said, *'Gentlemen, I ain't a goin'*'" (display's emphasis). The final statement on the poster describes how hectic and quick the shoot-out was: "Gunfire, chaos, and death ensued [. . .] **All in a moment**" (display's emphasis).

Surrounding the display, there are pictures and other ephemera, mostly photographs that appeared in the newspapers at the time. From left to right, we get pictures of the participants, including the Allen family and county officials. The description "Baldwin Felts Take Charge" is seen below, along with more pictures from the newspapers of the time. To the very right of the poster, it shows the mugshots of the Allen men. The arrangement of these materials is similar to the collage discussed earlier, located above the wooden carving. This arrangement, while sometimes hard to decipher, presents a vernacular remembering of the shoot-out. The story is made richer by having Bill Webb there to fill in the gaps. Webb goes into detail about the Allen family and their arrests, making an effort to scoff at the media depictions of the event and to focus on the interpersonal lives of the Allens.

The basis of the story is on the peg board, but the shoot-out exhibit focuses almost entirely on Hillsville's role in the shoot-out and does not broaden out to the region of Appalachia. Instead, the exhibit includes local newspaper articles that offer local retellings about the Allens and their progeny. The first one, "John Farris Is Last

Living Member of Famous Courthouse Tragedy," is from the *Carroll News*. Below that article is the grave inscription for Floyd and Claude's original tombstone, and right above that is J. Sidna Allen's obituary from the *Carroll News*. The inclusion of these three articles highlights the local presence of these exhibitions and their focus on humanizing instead of exploiting the participants of the shoot-out. The tombstone and the obituary display sympathy toward the Allen side. J. Sidna Allen's obituary is included because he, Floyd, and Claude were the top three men in the media; these articles are meant to displace the earlier stereotypical depictions of the men and replace them with historic ones. The tombstone is included because of its cultural significance in the town's lore.

J. Sidna Allen's woodwork, the courtroom carvings, Jezebel's medal, and the peg board are all examples of how the Carroll County Historical Society and Museum uses local narratives to retell the story of the courthouse shoot-out. The woodwork and the peg board both favor the Allen side, portraying the Allen men not as criminals but as sympathetic contributors to the shoot-out. On the other hand, much like the two memorials in the historic courthouse, the Goad medal is an attempt to show the town's side of the shoot-out.

"The Story of the Century": The Mount Airy Museum of Regional History

Unlike the courthouse museum, the Mount Airy Museum of Regional History, established in 1993, contains an attempt at official history through a small display on the second floor of the museum; however, the display sensationalizes the event using masculine violence. While the museum does try to humanize the Allen men, the exhibit fails because it overreaches by depending on the stereotypes rendered in the newspapers. The museum's website explains how the museum's main focus is to tell stories about the region:

> Ours is an all American story—typical of how communities grew up all across our great nation. While our story takes place in the back country of northwestern North Carolina at the foot of the Blue Ridge Mountains, it is likely to bear many similarities to the development of crossroads, towns, and cities throughout America[9]

The description combines the Appalachian identity with a developing America. This is an epideictic moment that celebrates the ways in which mountain life is an "all American story." It wants to conflate both identities using ideas of the life of the pioneer, which is alluded to *several* times throughout the museum in earlier well-funded exhibits. Their glass cases and name plates are sponsored by donations.[10] These displays are interactive and contain buttons patrons can push to hear an automated voice talk about the exhibit. Despite the expensive, impressive displays, the story of the Hillsville shoot-out is told on a board covered in carpet. In contrast to the Carroll County Historical Society and Museum's exhibit, this museum carefully outlines the participants in the shoot-out. The story is very carefully and implicitly told by this display using subtitles and pictures. It is made official because it is in a federally funded museum; however, the display remains somewhat vernacular because it contains artifacts such as newspaper clippings throughout.

Unlike the courthouse museum, there is no guide here to present the story of the shoot-out to patrons. They must construct the story using the materials that the exhibit presents. Organized in a chronological manner, these materials tell a story that places Hillsville in the Appalachian region and Appalachia within the national identity of America.

The introduction slide sets the scene: "No single event in the twentieth century received more news coverage in area newspapers, nor sparked more conversation and heated debate than did the courthouse tragedy that happened in nearby Carroll County, Virginia on

March 14, 1912." Mentioning the media prepares patrons for all the newspapers clippings they are about to see. It demonstrates the stereotypical, violent mountaineer rhetorical remembering discussed in chapter 1.

Next, the display gives an overview of the shoot-out and those involved, and it describes the governor's call to send troops to "quell the insurrection." The introduction continues as follows: "This story is filled with intrigue involving blockaders, money, politics, power, romance, and social injustice. Nearly 94 years after its occurrence the story remains an open book, with the final chapter yet to be written." This excerpt not only offers patrons buzzwords of interest but also represents the social and economic class of the Allen men and those in the courthouse. It also notes that the museum created this exhibit in 2006.

The introduction ends with a call for action to the viewers: "This Photo-Journalism exhibit is presented with one purpose in mind—the viewer to ponder the times, the circumstances with the relativity to our society today." Like the courthouse museum, many of the pictures in the exhibit came from local and national papers of the time. By using these images, this exhibit depends on the media portrayal of the violent mountaineer and uncivilized other, especially as it relates to the local Mount Airy newspaper.

In a section titled "The Setting," the curators decide to start by showing "normal" life in Hillsville and then how the Allens veered from that life to become moonshiners. There is not even a threat of violence here, but just a sign. The introductory sentence casts Hillsville as a sleepy little town with a population of about five hundred. The narrative continues, "In 1912, [Hillsville] would hardly seem the likely setting for a massacre." The use of the word *massacre* here mirrors the use of *tragedy* earlier; both words reveal the local government side and the Allen side.[11] Using the word *shoot-out* would be much more objective, but their acknowledgment of both sides demonstrates that the curators are knowledgeable about the trauma the event still has on the people of Hillsville. The display continues to elaborate on the curators' knowledge with the following:

> People lived life doing the everyday things people do as reflected in the photograph on the left of the Hillsville General Store. Two other photographs tell a different, darker story of Hillsville, Virginia. Notice the warning message expressed in the top photograph, 'Don't Go This Path' leading to Floyd Allen's moonshine still. The lower photograph shows evidence gathered of making illegal liquor. Though the Allen Family always denied making moonshine, legal records show raids on their property indicated that they did.

This piece of text turns the story again from the "normal" life of people in the mountains to the scandalous, dangerous, violent mountaineer rhetorical remembering. It distinguishes the Allen family as something out of the norm—a family that will not be forced to fit the values of progressive America. Ironically, both Floyd and J. Sidna Allen owned successful stores in and around Hillsville and were successful businessmen, and so they fit rather well into the ideal of economic progress that was prevalent in America at the time.[12]

Interestingly, the exhibit has numerous descriptions of J. Sidna Allen, his home, his family, and his reformation/craftsmanship, but it offers very little about Floyd Allen. The descriptions that we get of Floyd are the stereotypical outlaw rememberings that occur in the newspaper clippings in and around the exhibit. The focus on J. Sidna Allen leads viewers to believe that he was sorry for his crimes. The only significant information available on both Floyd and Claude is on the tombstones that occur later in the exhibit. It illustrates the lives J. Sidna and Floyd Allen led after the shoot-out and the penance that they had to pay for their crimes.

The middle panel introduces the characters of the shoot-out. Pictures of Floyd Allen, J. Sidna Allen, Claude Allen, Friel Allen,

Wesley Edwards, Sidna Edwards, Victor Allen, and Byrd Marion are above pictures of the new and old courthouse. Again, J. Sidna Allen is featured in this part of the display. A picture of his house is included, and he is described as "one of the wealthiest men in Hillsville." Floyd Allen's modest home is also pictured. In addition, the sections of the exhibit titled "The Courtroom" and "The Gunfight" present pictures of those who died as well as a schema of the courtroom. Like the wooden carving in the courthouse museum, these sections illustrate the moment of the shoot-out, and the schema specifically provides scientific proof of how the shots were fired and how each person was maimed or killed. Finally, Betty Ayers, who was "shot one time, killed," is mentioned. This mere mention of Betty Ayers demonstrates that this coverage of the shoot-out is still mostly masculine and embedded in violence.

The panel called "The Hunt" focuses on the Baldwin–Felts Detective Agency and its role in tracking down the Allen men after the shoot-out, engaging with the outlaw, violent mountaineer rhetorical remembering. It presents numerous pictures of the posse that left Hillsville, shows places where the Allen men could have hidden, and even includes an image of the hounds that helped track the Allen men. There are also wanted posters and pictures of J. Sidna and Friel Allen. In addition, this panel presents a newspaper clipping that shows an injured Floyd being carried out of the hotel where he was taken after being shot on Main Street. This picture was taken shortly after he supposedly tried to take his life by cutting his own throat (as seen in the bandage on his neck in the picture). As with the contemporary media of the time, this panel strives to tell an exciting story about the chase and capture of the Allens. While these images depict the Allens as outlaws, engaging with the violent mountaineer rhetorical remembering, the next panels titled "The Trials" and "The Sentences" present a sense of justice. These panels depict the public's reception of the trials with pictures of the crowds gathered around J. Sidna Allen and Wesley Edwards as they went to court. They also include pictures of the juries from each of their trials. The inclusion of these pictures provide closure. In this way, the exhibit focuses on the judicial aspect of shoot-out, while the other museums do not.

The section titled “The Aftermath” focuses on the final moments of Floyd, Claude, and J. Sidna Allen in an attempt to humanize them much like the courthouse museum tries to do. There is a picture of Floyd and Claude’s funeral procession. Below it is an image of the headstone that still remains on the grave today. Below that picture is the gravestone that has since disappeared but is rumored to still be with the Allen family. These also provide closure to the outlaw images displayed earlier.

To the right of the Floyd and Claude pictures and above their markers is a picture of J. Sidna Allen in a chair, with his arm on one of his homemade tables. Much like how he is portrayed in the courthouse museum, the rest of the exhibit presents the reformed version of him. Below his picture, curators wrote,

> J. Sidna Allen was pardoned in 1926 by Virginia Governor Harry F. Byrd. On the advice of friends, he decided not to return to Carroll County. Rather, he went to stay with an older brother, Victor, who was living in Leaksville (Rockingham County), North Carolina. In the 1930s, he moved to Mount Airy where he lived until 1941. Later that same year, due to sickness, he went to live with a daughter in Carroll County where he died on September 26, 1941.

While we see Floyd and Claude’s funeral and their gravestones, these words show patrons a calmer, more stoic figure who can no longer live in Hillsville. We do *not* hear about how Betty Allen, his wife, continued to live in Hillsville and provided for their two daughters by cleaning houses and doing laundry for those in town. We clearly see the continuation of the masculine depictions of the shoot-out. The only mention of the women is the reference to J. Sidna Allen's daughter, whom he moved in with at the end of his life. Their story is not important in the retelling of the shoot-out in the exhibit; rather, the importance lies only in the portrayal of J. Sidna Allen, who decorated his home in Mount Airy with a stone wall and is a renowned craftsman.

The last two parts of this panel are two pieces of text that demonstrate that this history contains some vernacular histories and that there is a valuable commodity attached to the shoot-out. The first piece of text states, "The Mountain Airy Museum of Regional History would like to thank Ron Hall, Steve Talley, Rossie George and Angela Schmoll for their assistance with the photo exhibit 'Story of the Century.'" To the uninformed patron, these names could just be the people who helped put the exhibit together, but those who know the history of the shoot-out know that Hall is the author of *The Carroll County Courthouse Tragedy* and is considered to be *the* informant about the shoot-out. He, more than likely, contributed to the exhibit through telling his version of the story. This explanation leads to the next section of text, which gives brief descriptions of Hall's book and J. Sidna Allen's memoir and dates the 1912 editions of the *Mount Airy News* that are included in the display. The text tells patrons that copies of the books are for sale in the museum shop. This is important because promoting the books in the exhibit encourages visitors to do their own primary research on the shoot-out, just like the exhibit and gift shop at the courthouse museum do. It also helps patrons support the museum and local historians.

The last text on the board and to the right of "The Aftermath" section is a quick response (QR) code that guides readers to an article that appeared in the *Roanoke Times* in November 1982. This QR code is an attempt to keep the exhibit updated; however, the link doesn't add much to the retelling of the event. More QR codes do exist in other exhibits throughout the museum, so placing one here indicates that the curators find this exhibit valuable (but not valuable enough to keep updated). Again, this asks patrons to interact with the exhibit and create their own vernacular history of the event.

Besides the carpeted exhibit, there is a glass-covered exhibit that houses two keys from the Hillsville jailhouse as well as the jailhouse in Floyd County and a special issue from the *Mount Airy Leader* from March 1912. These items contribute to a "local" story of the shoot-out. Next to these artifacts are two boxes that Wesley Edwards made. While the courthouse museum placed J. Sidna Allen's pieces first, this museum chooses to put these pieces by Wesley last. Representing the "final chapter yet to be written" mentioned in the exhibit's introductory statements, putting Wesley's artifacts at the end is a nod to tradition and learning. Wesley learned woodworking from his uncle while in the penitentiary. Interestingly, they both were Masons; the Mason moon and star are still found atop J. Sidna Allen's house, on the box he made that is on display at the courthouse museum, and on one of the boxes that Wesley made, which can be seen in this display. It distinctly says "From Wesley" on the box as well. Displaying his work here signifies Wesley's reformation and penance for his crimes. It's a nod to Appalachian craftsmanship but also a glimpse of the future of the Allen men. Unlike J. Sidna Allen, Wesley Edwards was only twenty-one years old during the shoot-out and was pardoned in 1923 at the age of thirty-two. He lived until 1939.[13] Furthermore, during my visit in 2022, a museum staff member told me that they were reconstructing the exhibit to include a model of the J. Sidna Allen House. This addition would reinforce the portrayal of them both as talented woodworkers instead of violent men.

Through these remembrances, the Mount Airy Museum of Regional History presents an organized historical look at the shoot-out that still relies on the rhetorical remembering of mountain violence to tell the story. The exhibit attempts to couch the history and identity of Appalachia within the shoot-out; however, it only does so in ways that turn to the same masculine violence that was depicted in the courthouse museum. Instead of depicting Appalachia as a developing region and the Allen men as businessmen in the area, the curators depend on the images of the Appalachian moonshiner and violent mountaineer to pull patrons into the story. The Allens are once again rendered as sensationalized outlaws who shot up the courthouse and paid for their outlaw behavior.

Cowboy Boots, a Two-Headed Calf, and Artifacts from the Shoot-Out: The Harmon Museum

The third site is the Harmon Museum, which, like the previous two museums, utilizes the violent mountaineer rhetorical remembering. It literally depends on the media stereotypes to tell the story of the shoot-out, along with other ephemera that is supposedly connected to the event. To consider this site a museum would be a stretch because it is Gooch Harmon's personal archive; however, it still operates as a site of public memory where a certain rhetorical memory of the shoot-out is created. To enter the museum, patrons have to walk through the lobby of Harmon's store, past shelves of cowboy boots and racks of Western shirts, then down a short hallway to a dimly lit room. Much like the other museums, the hallway houses local historical books about the shoot-out and other local and regional histories that patrons can buy. Entering the museum, patrons see the shoot-out memorabilia on the right. Other exhibits include a Native American artifact collection, a stone collection, a pioneer-style fireplace surrounding by farming equipment, and even a stuffed two-headed calf. Despite the varied presentation of artifacts, the Harmon Museum contains probably one of the most expansive displays about the shoot-out. It spans for two aisles and contains a wealth of newspaper articles, framed family pictures, framed pictures of the surrounding areas, and other artifacts. While these exhibits are under glass, they most certainly create an informal telling of the shoot-out. It offers visitors the chance to peruse the articles at their leisure and to construct their own views on it. While this collection is organized into certain areas, as I mentioned above, each is cluttered with *so much* information it is often overwhelming. When approaching this archive, my analysis will look at how these artifacts depict an epideictic history that constructs a certain rhetorical remembering of the event.

These artifacts represent a materialistic view of the shoot-out—one that wants viewers to gawk at things that were actually there or are associated with the history of the event. The speculative nature of the museum allows patrons to have a tangible thing to witness. The first thing that patrons will notice is the sheer number of artifacts here. There are artifacts ranging from Floyd Allen's saddlebags and Wesley Edwards's hat to artist Vernon Dalhart's vinyl album of the ballad "Sydny Allen."

As noted, the biggest part of this collection is the newspapers. Harmon has collected numerous issues of local and national newspapers pertaining to the event, and he displays them chronologically. Each issue is under glass, prompting patrons to *slow down* to read about the event. Visitors are able to pick and choose what they want to read about the event. While it's good that the articles are under glass, they are by no means preserved in a manner that would satisfy an archivist. The fluorescent lights over the glass will lead to further deterioration of the articles, but the fact that Harmon has them preserved under glass and not touchable is worth noting. Through doing so, he is attempting to preserve the artifacts in the best way he and whoever continues to curate the museum knows how.

By preserving the newspapers, curators continue to contribute to the violent retelling of the shoot-out; however, the display on the Baldwin–Felts Detective Agency overtly demonstrates his slant toward law and order. At the end of the expansive newspaper trail on the shoot-out, patrons see in bright yellow "Baldwin Felts Detectives" on a display board and "T.L. Felts Six Scrap Books" written on the case below. The case contains pieces from Felts's scrapbook, a hat, pistols, and a wooden box, among other personal items. On the display board, Harmon placed pictures of the Baldwins and Felts. The showcase not only focuses on the Allens and the shoot-out but also gives another glimpse into the Baldwin–Felts Detective Agency, characterizing the detectives as lawful heroes. The inclusion of these materials asks observers to believe in the justice and honor of the Baldwin–Felts Detective Agency, which is the complete opposite of showing sympathy to the Allens. This display is indeed one of law and order, further acknowledging John Bodnar's point that objects in public spaces "can even clash with one another."[14] What is missing from the display is the cruelty of the nature of the Baldwin–Felts Detective Agency. There is little evidence of their terrible role in the Matewan disaster or their activity in any of the Coal Wars that were also happening in the Appalachians shortly after the shoot-out. We see here that the vernacular retelling showcases their role as a detective agency and *not* as coal mining town gun thugs.

While the Harmon Museum does carry a bigger volume of materials than the other two museums, it is the retelling of the event that is overwhelming. Unlike the chronological, chosen pieces for both the courthouse museum and the Mount Airy museum, Harmon puts *all* of his artifacts out on display, giving patrons the opportunity to choose for themselves what they want to learn about the shoot-out. There is no official designation to his museum (except for the big sign that says museum outside his store). Harmon relies solely on the stereotypical rememberings of the shoot-out through newspapers and artifacts that evoke the violent mountaineer. While this way of retelling the event is interesting because of the personal touches like Floyd's saddlebags, it is also biased because it tells his *own* version of the story, as seen in the one-sided documentation of the Baldwin–Felts Detective Agency.

Conclusion

Visiting each of these museums reveals how curators rhetorically remember the event. Through epideictic artifacts they construct specific rhetorical rememberings by emphasizing certain cultural values they deem important. Each display shows how the event is powered by vernacular retellings that are conveyed not only orally but also in writing, such as in newspaper articles. While the town is conflicted about the representations of its citizens in the media, news articles are still used to depict the history of the shoot-out. In addition, the emphasis on J. Sidna Allen at the Mount Airy Museum of Regional History demonstrates how curators choose who to focus on in their displays. With the gradual uptake of technology, such as the Friends of the J. Sidna Allen House Facebook group, places of public memory will continue to evolve to become even more vernacular-based instead of government-sanctioned. Local photographer Rita Edlein's photographs of the J. Sidna Allen House and the performance of Frank Levering's plays in the old courthouse demonstrate how these spaces are now used as more than merely a place to memorialize the events that took place there. They now function as places where art is created. These new uses will only add to the continued retelling of the story of the shoot-out, a story that, like these museums, is vernacularly official.

Returning to the historic J. Sidna Allen House in 2016, I sit at a large table in the dining room while it rains outside. It is me, two actors from the recent Levering plays, and another couple who attended the media event earlier in the day. Stu Shenk, who portrays J. Sidna Allen in the play, recounts J. Sidna Allen's story—how he came to wealth, the shoot-out, and a brief history of his house. Kay Cox, who plays Betty Allen in the play, interjects frequently with Betty's role in the shoot-out. Their retelling of the story in the historic home reminds me of the power of the history of the shoot-out.

It not only resides in these places and artifacts of public memory, but is retold through generations of residents, and often descendants of the people from the shoot-out. There is indeed power in the retelling of the story. It is a power that privileges certain sides, depending on who is telling the story. But perhaps the most important thing that I realized after visiting the house and hearing Kay's frequent interjections is what is *not* recorded in the museums nor in the history of the shoot-out—the voices of the women who were left behind and continued to tell the story.

"I Wish You Had Not Thought to Come Here"

Feminine Silences, Pleas, and Community Rhetorics from the 1912 Hillsville, Virginia, Courthouse Shoot-Out

> [. . .] countering apathy and the paralysis of anger and cynicism. Rhetorical empathy [balances] and sustains. There is a place for both critique and repair [. . .]
>
> Lisa Blankenship in *Changing the Subject: A Theory of Rhetorical Empathy*[1]

She was known as the "woman in woe," wearing black garb when she appeared in newspaper articles. Both her husband and son were found guilty of shooting up the courthouse in the small mountain town of Hillsville, Virginia, and so they were executed by the state. Publicly, she remained silent except for one letter she submitted to the local newspaper, asking for money after her barn and all the valuables in it mysteriously burned to the ground. She had no money, and her other sons could only do so much for her.

Over one hundred years later, her silence is broken when a local playwright gives her a voice. She is Frances Allen, wife to Floyd Allen. Frances, her sister-in-law Betty Allen, Jezebel Goad (the daughter of Dexter Goad, the clerk of court, who was injured during the shoot-out), and Maude Iroler (Wesley Edwards's girlfriend) all are silent in the rememberings of the shoot-out. In fact, in all of the popular depictions of the shoot-out, the women of Hillsville are only briefly mentioned, until recently.

Where were these women's stories? Why were they missing in the public retellings of the story? How did they put their lives back together after such a traumatic event?

To answer these questions, the rich narratives of women's voices must be recovered in light of the dominant, violent, male-centered rememberings of the event. They are critically important because their "her-stories" tell audiences the complete story of the shoot-out. These stories reveal a new remembering, one that focuses on not just the men involved but also the widows, wives, and children left at home after the traumatic incident. However, in the coverage of the news media, we see a story that is not told truthfully. These historical rhetorical rememberings of the shoot-out involve false reporting—or what has now been so popularly referred to as "fake news"— about Jezebel Goad and Betty Allen. The media claimed that Jezebel heroically helped her father, Dexter Goad (the clerk of court), by reloading his pistol during the shoot-out. Soon after, the governor and his wife had a medal cast for Jezebel in her honor. As seen earlier, the Carroll County Historical Society and Museum tells the story in their exhibit about the fictional event, further participating in the false masculine retelling by having her participate in the violence that the men created during the shoot-out. Another newspaper article notes that Betty Allen, J. Sidna Allen's wife and Floyd's sister-in-law, was killed during another dramatic shoot-out at their Victorian home. Neither of these events actually happened but were written to produce more dramatic frenzy around the shoot-out.[2] Meanwhile, we do see direct action by Maude Iroler, who led the Baldwin–Felts Detective Agency to J. Sidna Allen and Wesley Edwards but also refused to participate in interviews, much like Jezebel.

While these "fake news" articles operate as rhetorical rememberings and made these women popular to the public, analyzing the women's historical responses is critical to understanding why they largely remained silent about the event. Their responses reveal the true nature of each woman's approach to the shoot-out. They also contradict the rhetorical reconstruction of these memories and instead solely rely on the historical facts of each woman's experience. Many years after the shoot-out, Jezebel and Maude both were approached to talk about their role in the tragedy. Instead of perpetuating the masculine violence as portrayed in the media, they stayed silent and chose not to tell their story. Right after the shoot-out and soon after the false shoot-out article, Betty Allen chose to quietly misguide the Baldwin–Felts agents and the media by giving them an old picture of her husband while he was hiding from authorities. Frances Allen, the woman in woe, admitted that she needed help financially for lawyers for her husband and son. Lastly, Maude Iroler, who is only represented in the media and in J. Sidna Allen's autobiography (but not in any museum), is pivotal in the shoot-out because she is the one who eventually aided in the capture of J. Sidna Allen and Wesley Edwards. Each of these responses warrants investigation and further analysis because they signify the women's roles in participating or *not* participating in the story of the shoot-out.

While historically, these women did not participate in the shoot-out, I argue that local playwright Frank Levering's *Thunder in the Hills* recovers these voices and brings them front and center on the stage not only to empower these women, but also to present what Lisa Blankenship deems rhetorical empathy toward both sides of the shoot-out. While Levering writes as a male writer with his own biases, these fictional portrayals still present a rhetorical remembering of the women in the shoot-out where they are active members in the events. Sadly, Jezebel Goad and Maude Iroler are missing from the play, but both Frances and Betty Allen depict empathetic characters whom the audience can connect to and feel sympathetic toward. The character of Frances dominates much of the play, and her overwhelming guilt and angst is brought forward to finally give the community an idea of the suffering on *both* sides of the shoot-out—the

Allen men and the local government. In addition, Levering's construction of the play involves local actors and actresses who are family of those involved in the shoot-out. Involving family members, performing the play in the historic courthouse, and using rhetorical empathy to unearth these women's voices presents a new rhetorical remembering of the shoot-out that portrays both sides equally and shuns the portrayals in the media as well as the museums' feckless, stereotypical Appalachian violence.

Resurrecting Voices: Methodology

While I looked through the archives in the Library of Virginia and talked to community members in Hillsville, I realized that these women's voices should be recovered. I have made a genuine effort to allow the women to speak for themselves as much as possible. In fact, for much of the research done for this chapter, I rely on local Hillsville scholar Shelby Puckett's presentation titled "Aftermath of the Courthouse Tragedy," which she presented at the Centennial Symposium in Hillsville, Virginia, in 2012. There are places, however, where I have had to rely on male-written speculation, such as newspapers, nonfiction writing such as J. Sidna Allen's memoirs, and Levering's plays to construct my argument.

Engaging with empathetic rhetorics and archival research presents a reciprocal reading between the archive and theory, one which feminist archivist scholars Cheryl Glenn and Jessica Enoch note "permits theory to speak to archival finds and archival finding to push against, open up, question, extend, constrict, or even disregard the theoretical frame altogether. In other words, the reading and the theory inform each other."[3] These archived women's voices will indeed open the retelling of the shoot-out and raise tensions and perspectives in ways that were not evident in the museums. Similar to the archival reciprocities, these artifacts and the presentations in the plays engage with rhetorical empathy. As Lisa Blankenship describes, "it's initiated by the speaker or writer toward an audience and ideally reciprocated by the audience in return, often as a result of the audience being treated with dignity rather than as a stereotype or with (often justifiable) anger."[4] Furthermore, tension is apparent in the women's silence regarding the shoot-out itself as they present empathetic views of themselves. Both Frances and Jezebel write emotional letters that convey their different approaches to the shoot-out. As readers, we can empathize, especially after knowing the full history of the shoot-out. In addition, the portrayals of Frances and Betty in the plays treat their characters with dignity but also demonstrate an empathetic retelling of the narrative that evokes emotion. The uncovering and presentation of these women's voices, particularly in these dramatic representations, produce pity and compassion not only for the women involved but also for all the lives that were affected by the shoot-out. These retellings create a *new* narrative that doesn't stop after the death of Floyd and Claude Allen.

"Very Distasteful to Me": Historical, Traumatic Silences, Reactions, and Pleas for Help

As mentioned in the previous chapter, the Carroll County Historical Society and Museum in the historic courthouse is one of the only museums that houses a display on one of the women in the shoot-out—Jezebel Goad. In the exhibit, a gold medal, the mold for the medal, a letter from Governor Mann, and his wife's memoir celebrate the false actions of Jezebel in the shoot-out. Jezebel was the daughter of the clerk of court, Dexter Goad, who (in Floyd Allen's words) was the "sworn enemy of the Allens."[5] Ironically, Dexter Goad's portrait and law degree loom high above Jezebel's exhibit, which inadvertently reminds visitors that masculine violence contributed to the shoot-out.

A news report at the time claimed that Jezebel came to the rescue of her father by loading his pistol by his side during the shoot-out. In today's vernacular, this incident would most certainly be qualified as "fake news." In this case, the media created the false report, which was then picked up by the governor of Virginia and his wife, much like some of the immediate reactions to today's news media. In response to this coverage by the paper, Governor Mann sent Jezebel a letter as well as a medal inscribed with the words "Tribute of Honor [. . .] for Heroic Courage in Defense of Justice, Hillsville, VA March 14, 1912" and "A Brave and Devoted Daughter."

Through these statements on the medal, the governor notes that the men are "brave," but that that type of behavior is not expected from the women of Hillsville. In addition, Etta Donnan Mann, the governor's wife, writes in her memoir not only about Jezebel's role, but also about the loss of Nancy Elizabeth "Betty" Ayers, who was a witness who died the next day after the shoot-out:

> March 15th Today a woman witness for the Allen faction, Betty Ayers, succumbed to wounds that she really didn't know she had received, and one of the jurors died from injuries received during the fight yesterday in the courthouse. A brave defense was made by the Clerk of the Court, Dexter Goad, who, although wounded, fought to the bitter end, firing away all his ammunition and following the gang out of the courthouse. His daughter, the Deputy-Clerk, evinced the greatest bravery, assisting her father and handing him more ammunition when all of his was gone[6]

The book does bring the tragedy of Betty Ayers's death to the forefront; however, her death is eclipsed by the heroic acts of Jezebel assisting her father during the shoot-out.

Despite Mann's letters and medal and his wife's writing, Jezebel did *not* help her father reload his pistol. In Floyd's trial on Friday, May 3, 1912, which started at 9:30 a.m., Dexter Goad was questioned by Judge N. H. Hairston for the defense:

Q: You say your daughter came in there. Did she bring you a pistol?
A: No, sir, she did not.
Q: So the publication was a mistake?
A: Yes, sir, the publication was a mistake.

However, as Bill Lord notes in his book *Red Ear of Corn*, Dexter Goad denies this statement: "In later years, however, he often remarked, yes, Jezebel did give him a gun, 'and it worked like a charm.'"[7] There are *still* rumors that Jezebel contributed to the shoot-out, as seen on the Library of Virginia's website.[8] Her actual appearance at the shoot-out is insignificant. The real interest is the desire for the media and public memory to regard her as a folk hero for supposedly helping her father. The only mentions of her are written on paper and told orally. Her status as the sole woman in the shoot-out is inconsequential and rendered a moot point since it is false.

In contrast to the fictional Jezebel's violent action, we actually see the historical Jezebel Goad asserting action in her defiance to participate in the retelling of the shoot-out; an account that does *not* occur in the museum's remembrance of the event. In 1965, Don Murray, the news director at WDBJ Television of Roanoke, Virginia, wanted to do a segment that showcased the shoot-out. Murray asked Senator Floyd Landreth, who was the special prosecutor in the trials, to ask Jezebel if she would like to be included in the program. Jezebel's response to Landreth is terse, short, and it shows how much she did *not* want to talk about the shoot-out. Her letter reads as follows:

> Dear Floyd: I have your letter of April 30th in regard to the WDBJ Television Program relating to the Allen Tragedy. I am sorry but I do not wish to comply with your request as it would be very distasteful to me. It is a subject [that] I have tried to forget and which I never discuss with anyone. Anyway, I have forgotten so many of the details that it would not be of any interest to the public except those of morbid curiosity. Therefore, I do [not] wish to discuss, reminisce, nor rehearse the affair for

> public consumption. I am sorry. With all my best wishes to you, Sincerely yours, Jezebel Goad[9]

Jezebel's insistence that silence is important is evident in her refusal to retell the story. There is clearly a "not" implied after the "do" in the letter. From this we can see that her rhetorical purpose is polite and rejects the gun-loading heroine the press made her out to be. Unlike Betty or Frances, who do not articulate their silence surrounding the event, Jezebel finds it "distasteful" to talk about. Cheryl Glenn in *Unspoken: A Rhetoric of Silence* writes that the most important use of silence is for users to "fulfill their rhetorical purpose, whether it is to maintain their position of power or resist the domination of others."[10] She continues by stating the following:

> The power of language itself, however, can yield silence in cases where words and actions are used to impose silence on someone else or to suggest silence as the best tact for someone else. Thus, those who embrace silence in these situations do so for psychological and intentional purposes. That person must remain silent or be hurt in some way, some emotional, intellectual, physical, or professional way. The silencer dominates the silenced, once again gendering the conditions of speaking and silence.[11]

By refusing to participate in the "public consumption" of the shoot-out, Jezebel maintains control over her narrative of the event. Her silence implies that she is the one who knows the "true" story of what happened. Her notions that she has "tried to forget" the shoot-out but also has "forgotten so many of the details" suggest that she still remembers the trauma suffered there but retains the right to talk about it on her own terms—her deliberate silence acts as a powerful rhetorical (in)action.

While Jezebel is considered a folk hero who defended her father, the museum visitors are not informed that Betty Allen, J. Sidna Allen's wife, led the detectives away from her husband during the manhunt. Betty economically suffered the most because their house was attached to the trial, and they lost it after the shoot-out. She moved into town and did laundry and cleaned for the townspeople to provide for their daughters. The first winter in Hillsville was particularly cold, and there are reports that they suffered greatly during this time.[12] One of the first times we see Betty Allen as an active participant in the shoot-out is her fictional death in the newspapers. On March 16, 1912, an article titled "Two More Dead in Allen Feud" in the *New York Times* noted, "in a battle in which she was assisting her husband to resist arrest, the wife of Sidna Allen was instantly killed" and that J. Sidna Allen was "believed to be dying as the result of the wound received in yesterday's fray."[13] This reporter completely fabricates a gunfight that happened at their Victorian home, where Betty is killed trying to help her husband.[14] Similar to Jezebel, this depiction of Betty Allen shows that she is "assisting her husband" in the shoot-out. The reporter portrays her as violent and, like the other victims of the shoot-out, she falls victim to that violence. While these descriptions are clearly *not* true, Betty did, in fact, intentionally help her husband as he fled to Iowa.

After the shoot-out, when the Baldwin–Felts Detective Agency came to her to get a picture of her husband so they could find him during the manhunt, Betty misguided them by presenting an old picture instead of a more recent one. By misrepresenting her husband, she distracted the detectives as he and her nephew escaped to Iowa. This simple act allowed them more time to get settled. Betty's old picture of J. Sidna Allen is run in all the newspapers that depict him as the ringleader of the Allen men. Her manipulation of the detectives is clearly not as active as her role in the fictional shoot-out; however, I would argue that it is just as important since she did slow down the detectives during the search for her husband.

Opposing Jezebel's silence and Betty's actions, Frances Allen suffered differently during the event that led to the deaths of both her husband and her son. She was an orphan when Floyd met her. After they married, they lost their first child from fever at age five. Next, they had Victor, and then Claude, whom she "doted over."[15] Frances was particularly proud of Claude because he went to business school in Raleigh, North Carolina, then returned home to help his parents with the farm. This further disrupts many popular stereotypes of the Allen men. During the shoot-out, Frances was fifty-four years old, but she appears much older in newspaper photographs.

During the trial and afterward, the media depicted Frances Allen as weak and mournful. Frances became known as the "woman in woe" and the "lady in black" after the deaths of her husband and son. Throughout the trials, Frances "sat without saying anything and tears would roll down her face."[16] She visited the men frequently while they were in jail, always appearing sickly or weak. Floyd's own words indicate that his wife was indeed sick. In his final statement in prison, he wrote, "This trouble, of course, is awfully hard on my wife. No man has ever had a better wife than I have. Her health has been bad and she has not been well for some time, and I know that her suffering is something awful."[17] He is rumored to have gotten emotional in the jail when talking about how hard Frances's life was and how the trial affected her. Frances was *not* allowed to attend the execution of the two men. At the funeral, Frances held Claude's body at the grave and wept. It is reported that she didn't even look at Floyd's casket. After the shoot-out, she moved with her son Victor to New Jersey where they both lived until her death in 1944. Per Puckett's accounts in her speech on the women in the shoot-out, Frances was known as a bitter woman who seldom spoke, but as Puckett notes in her talk, how could Frances be blamed for being bitter because of all the trauma that she had gone through during the trials and deaths of her son and husband?

Despite these depictions, Frances plays a large role in the advocacy of her husband and son in jail. In a letter written to the *Galax*

Post Herald on October 19, 1912, she articulates that her family wanted to pay for the trials of her son and husband.[18] This type of self-reliance is typical of the mountain family as they do not seek help from outside sources; however, in the letter, we do see her turning to the public after the family barn catches fire. The fire was more than likely caused by arson as tools were found stacked in a pile after the fire was put out. In addition, her thanking of the public echoes Floyd's own thanking of supporters who wrote in for his pardon: "I thank the Journal for the fight that they have made to save our lives. I also want to thank the papers in the State who have helped us and who have tried to give the true facts to the people of this and other States."[19] Their acknowledgement of the papers demonstrates the critical impact that these publications had on the trials of these two men. Because Frances is one of the two women from whom we actually hear, it is important to share her letter, in its totality, to hear her powerful and sympathetic voice:

> To the public
>
> The members of my family and our attorney have received many letters from persons offering to start public subscriptions to aid me in carry on the defense of my husband Floyd Allen and my son Claude Allen. We have refused these offers as we wanted to pay the expenses of these trials ourselves as long as we had anything to pay with. My husband and my two sons have gone through long and costly trials all summer that have taken all that we could raise on our home and during last summer our barn was burned without insurance while I was at Claude's trial in Wytheville and with it almost all the feed and farm machinery on the place. So that I have nothing to pay any further now. My husband and my boy are under death sentence and the appeals which our lawyers are preparing are expensive and we need money now because we have only a little over a month. If the people who have made these kind offers still want to help us anything they can collect and will send to me at Mount Airy, North Carolina will be used in the defense of my husband and

> my boy. I thank the many people who have written to me and have told me of their sympathy and their offers of help.
>
> Mrs. Frances Allen (as dictated by Puckett, Centennial speech)

The pardons that the public wrote for Claude more than likely inspired her to write this public outcry since this was published when the petitions started to appear in the media. These pardon letters are also found in the Library of Virginia archives, and they articulate quite clearly the empathy that some Virginians felt toward Floyd but especially Claude. Most of them see Claude as a folk hero who was trying to save his father. These hearken back to the romantic versions of Claude seen in the ballads in chapter 2. Despite these emotional letters, Frances wants to remain silent (much like Jezebel), but for her family's own well-being and financial security she cannot. Now functioning as the matriarch of the family, she must go to the public for help. She constructs a story of her husband and "boy" *not* as murderers but as two men who should be pardoned. She comes to us as a wife and mother pleading for our help; however, she is also trying to gain sympathy for herself. She has lost everything she owns and is about to lose her husband and son to the judicial system. She positions herself as the victim of her circumstances.

Perhaps one of the most controversial roles of women in the shoot-out is the role of Maude Iroler, who was Wesley Edwards's girlfriend at the time of the shoot-out. While Frances, Betty, and Jezebel are minor characters in the retelling of the shoot-out, Maude is a major player. She led the Baldwin–Felts Detective Agency to Des Moines, Iowa, which resulted in the capture of J. Sidna Allen and Wesley, ending the coverage of the event. Looking at her story and her role in the shoot-out, we notice that the ending of the shoot-out hinges on the creation of Maude as an innocent informant.

Maude's boyfriend, Wesley, was one of the two boys who fought in Garland Allen's church, which would lead to the trial with Floyd

Allen. Immediately after the shoot-out, Wesley fled to Des Moines, Iowa, with J. Sidna Allen to start a new life. During this time, Wesley kept in touch with Maude through letters and even a secret visit to Hillsville. During the visit, he exchanged money with Maude to ensure her passage so they could be together and get married. Maude's father found out about the money and supposedly made a deal with the Baldwin–Felts Detective Agency to follow her out there. The retelling of Maude's story and the capture of Wesley Edwards and J. Sidna Allen signify how the retelling of the story of the shoot-out *must* include Maude.

Seen in his memoirs, J. Sidna Allen's accounts reveal that he was none too pleased with Maude. He writes, "For a few hundred dollars she had betrayed both me and the man she promised to marry."[20] He continues, "He would talk very little to me about her. He knew what I thought about the whole matter. I felt sure she had betrayed us to the detectives. They say love is blind, so I suppose that accounted for his faith in her. I was informed by the detectives that she sold Wesley for five hundred dollars. Soon after her return to Virginia, she married another man."[21] He does say that he was excited to end his life of lies and be back with his wife and children, but we do see his bitterness over his capture. Maude's intervention in their capturing meant that he finally had to face justice for his role in the shoot-out.

While J. Sidna Allen is clearly adamant that Maude led to their capture, the media portrays Maude as mostly innocent. The *New York Times* on September 15, 1912, reports that "Wesley Edwards's sweetheart, Maude Iroler of Mount Airy, N.C., was the innocent cause of the arrest of the last of the clan for whom a country-wide search has been conducted." The article continues, "Little thinking that dogging her trail were four detectives" and how she was the "innocent cause of the betrayal of the whereabouts of Allen and Edwards, took their capture nonchalantly."[22] In "Allen Explains Shootout" on September 16, we continue to see that Maude "unconsciously gave the police the clue to their hiding place" but that she and Wesley "stoutly denied that the girl had deliberately betrayed Edwards. Detective Baldwin corroborated their statements. He said that when Edwards left Mount Airy, N.C., the girl's home, he had left $50 with her to be used to join him when he was safely secreted. The money was stolen and then replaced, and in this manner Miss Iroler's father learned of it."[23]

In the earlier article, though, we do get an impression of Maude as a headstrong young woman. She is "the daughter of Frank Iroler. She lived with her parents and has known the Allens, she says, since she was old enough to remember anything." We hear from Maude in this article as well as she states "'I just kind of got tired of staying at home. When Wesley was back there a short while ago he told me that I must come some time during this month.'" When asked if he visited his home she replied "'Why, yes, he was,' she replied firmly. 'I have known him longer than you, and it was then that we arranged that I was to come to Des Moines."[24] We see that Maude's expedition out west was to get out of Hillsville and to start a life of her own with Wesley. Her bravery and determination are to be noted as she traveled out west by herself to meet up with Wesley.

After the shoot-out, Maude had a successful life. She married Ken Marsh shortly after the trials of J. Sidna Allen and Wesley Edwards. Much like the other women, she didn't talk much about the event; however, according to Ronald W. Hall, she did agree to an interview (which wasn't recorded) with Ruth Minick, where Maude "admitted going to Des Moines with the detectives at her father's direction, putting to rest the years of rumors and theories about her part in the capture of the fugitives. She died September 19th, 1972."[25]

After J. Sidna Allen's comments, the media, and Maude's supposed interview with Minick, her innocence in leading to the capture of the Allen men is still questionable. Whether she was in cahoots with the Baldwin–Felts Detective Agency is irrelevant; rather, the issue is that she is included in *every* telling of the capture of the men. Maude signifies the end of the male-dominated violence. Much like Frances's refusal to talk, Betty's efforts to carry on with her life, and Jezebel's silence, Maude's intervention in the event leads to not only the men's capture but also normalcy.

These women's blatant refusal to talk directly about the shoot-out demonstrates their power over the narrative that the press continued to spin about the shoot-out. Their silence, actions, and pleas during the event and its related press coverage echo through the display in the courthouse museum because their voices are not there; however, when visitors ascend the stairs to the courthouse and see Frank Levering's plays performed, their silences are broken.

"Greedy for Guns and Blood": Recovered Women's Voices of Survival in Levering's *Thunder in the Hills*

In researching the shoot-out, members of the community are *still* unable to talk about it. Their ancestors' grief and trauma influence them even over a century later. Levering's plays offer these family members and other members of the town the opportunity to gather in the historic courthouse where the shoot-out happened and listen to the story together. The communal gathering, participation by audience members, and particular moments with the fictional characters of Frances and Betty Allen in the play enact what Lisa Blankenship deems rhetorical empathy. This empathy happens when community members open up to the possibility of sympathy just by being there with those who were on the other side of the shoot-out, depicted by the characters. Lisa Blankenship defines rhetorical empathy as

> both a topos and trope, a choice and habit of mind that invents and invites discourse informed by deep listening and its resulting emotion, characterized by narratives based on personal experience. Rhetorical empathy is both a hermeneutic and

> heuristic, a way of thinking (and feeling) constituted by language and a way of using language.[26]

Blankenship further explains that "empathy has signified an immersion in an Other's experience through verbal and visual artistic expression. This element of an immersive experience that results in an emotional response."[27] Blankenship's ideas on rhetorical empathy manifest in the play because the family members of those involved in the shoot-out are able to witness a fictional depiction of the events. They are able to see the women characters that Levering creates and see the humane side of these characters. Blankenship explains this exchange between the characters and audience members as a "rhetorical empathy [that] results in an emotional engagement that can disarm; it asks for vulnerability from the speaker or writer that can, at times, promote it in return."[28] This engagement indeed results in a disarming of the audience from their previous preconceived notions of their side of the shoot-out. The exchange leads to vulnerability and recognition of loss on both sides that, as many of the people who I talked to have said, has helped "heal the town." One of these aspects of exchange and healing was the use of the characters of Betty and Frances to humanize the shoot-out through the enactment of their experiences, which is much more effective than any of the museum's displays downstairs.

The spirited character of Betty, played by Kay Cox, is first introduced on the night before the shoot-out. Playing the foil to Frances Allen, Betty is full of zest and is willing to give her opinion. Her character is sexual, with lines like "Sidna hasn't thawed out yet [. . .] when I kiss him, his lips are still cold from being out west." (J. Sidna Allen earned his wealth by running a store in Alaska.) She also says, "Your brother loves his house more than the bedroom and me in the bed."[29] However, it's her calling out of the men that makes Betty's character important to the retelling of the tale. She tells Floyd on the night before the shoot-out, "You drag Sidna into this and I'll pull a gun on you myself."[30] This initial conversation with Betty is important because it establishes her as a prominent and spunky character. While Frances is often depicted as weak and unhealthy, Betty is portrayed as headstrong and not afraid to tell her truth—a truth that was mostly unheard before these plays were written and performed, except by family members. Whether this truth came from history or from Levering's creative mind, we still see a side of Betty that has never been presented.

Furthermore, Levering includes Betty's actions after the shoot-out. Betty states that she gave the detectives a fake picture that "looked more like Billy the Kid than Sidna Allen."[31] As mentioned before, this act is powerful because it exposes how Betty misguided the detectives. The fact that Levering includes this act shows that he knows the power of Betty's role in disrupting the manhunt for her husband. In addition, Levering includes the Billy the Kid reference here as a nod to the hillbilly/outlaw image that the media helped create.

In the same scene, Betty also mentions the newspaper article that said she was killed: "They said that Sidna's wife was killed in that battle. Well, I reckon they got me."[32] Betty's mention of this article is particularly important because it shows her sarcasm toward the complete and utter misguidance of the newspapers, and it prompts laughter from the audience when she talks about her own death. Knowing she did *not* die in the shoot-out (most audience members typically know about the shoot-out), the audience roars with laughter at this line; it is one of the biggest laughs in the play (as Kay, the actress, will tell you herself, like she told me when I heard her talk at the J. Sidna Allen House). Through her dialogue, Levering gives Betty a voice. She is not a solemn, mournful character like Frances, but rather she is an outspoken woman who isn't afraid to speak to men. She's not afraid to be sarcastic or to make jokes about the coverage of the shoot-out. Her deadpan honesty reveals that

Levering wants audiences to remember her as a strong-willed woman who had a hard life but was still able to survive despite her troubles. She is briefly seen at the end of the play when J. Sidna Allen is pardoned.

Besides the letter cited earlier, Frances was mostly quiet during the aftermath of the shoot-out. Depictions of her weeping in the courthouse at Floyd and Claude's trial and her dressing as the "woman in woe" dominate her media coverage. In his play, Levering creates a multidimensional persona for Frances. While she is not as plucky as Betty, Frances's character presents us with a sympathetic point of view. Her retelling indeed conveys the sadness, despair, and tragedy that was felt by numerous family members after the shoot-out. She gives us a perspective of the shoot-out that incorporates our morose speculation. She evokes pity and sympathy for the families that were left behind. Unlike Betty, Frances was *not* able to put her family back together, and she leaned heavily on her son Victor for support. Reading the beginning of Frances's speech and then her final statements in the play demonstrate feelings of morality and sympathy for those involved.

Frances starts with an invocation to the audience: "what do you want from me now [. . .] once ain't enough for you [. . .] greedy for guns and blood [. . .] you want to see folks shot, dead. That's what you're here for, trouble."[33] Levering's choice to start the play with Frances is important because she automatically hits us with guilt for wanting to see the traumatic incident replayed in the courthouse where it took place. *She* is the starting point of the story in this retelling. She acts as the storyteller, providing a moral and sympathetic outlook from the very first moments of the play. Her anger and sadness are palpable in Terri Ingalls's portrayal of Frances. She reminds us that, as eyewitnesses to the play, we can judge for ourselves "'Cause *you* are the jury."[34] This act is particularly powerful because, as seen in earlier archival material, Frances is silent through the trials, and a *woman* is presenting the tale to us, which has *not* occurred yet in all the retellings of the story of the shoot-out in a museum.

In the scene right before the shoot-out, we have a narrative jump in the play that is mostly told by Frances Allen. Even though this scene takes place the night before the shoot-out, Frances has visions of those killed in the shoot-out as they come to visit her when she is by herself at her home. (Floyd stayed that rainy night with his brother J. Sidna Allen.) These visions are fascinating not only because they foretell the shoot-out before it happens, but also because they happen to Frances and *not* her husband or son, who were in the courthouse during the shoot-out.[35] Levering gives Frances this dialogue and these visions to illustrate how emotionally distraught the shoot-out made her. Her silence is broken, and she is able to articulate the trauma that she suffered. She feels responsible for the violence that her son and husband caused. She is rendered useless in stopping the violence though.

In her visions, Frances refers to herself in the third person when she says, "[Wind] and rain like Noah's flood arising. What could Frances Allen do? Old before her time because it's gone back so fast. Death coming quick."[36] Frances already feels disconnected from the reality of the shoot-out. Her abrupt neurosis demonstrates the extreme trauma that she will endure in the next few days. In a time jump in the play, audience members watch as Betty Ayers, the only female victim from the shoot-out, comes to visit Frances from the grave, attempting to comfort her in a moment of compassion stating, "What was you going to do with the rest of your life?" to which Frances replies, "I have lost myself and there's no place for me deep down."[37] This exchange suggests that Frances has already sunk into a depression so deep that she can't even imagine herself dead, or in a more Christian interpretation, in hell, perhaps because she's already living it.

In her next exchange, however, we do see Frances strike back. When the ghost of Augustus Fowler (another victim of the shoot-out) visits, he points to where he died. Then, he states, "I got nothing against Floyd that we can't settle our accounts down yonder," gesturing that Floyd is in hell. Frances, in her grief and sorrow, reacts strongly, stating, "I ain't got no family [. . .] you leave this earth. You go farm in hell."[38] While this statement would obviously not be received well by the Fowler family, it shows Frances's frustration and anger over the shoot-out. She, in fact, yells back, "Where are the rest of you? Why won't you speak to me?" in an attempt to conjure up the rest of the victims for her either to seek penance from or to argue with.[39] Through these latter frustrations and visits with the dead, Frances works through her guilt over the killings. Although the redemption is lost on her (where it should have been bestowed on those who were actually at the shoot-out), we can see how these interactions had a profound influence on the way that Levering presents her reactions to the shoot-out.

After the reenactment of the shoot-out, Frances comes back on stage even though she was not there when the event happened. She states each person's name that died during the shoot-out, and each person leaves. Through her voice, the dead are memorialized and remembered solemnly in the courthouse. We do not hear from the men because they have already fled the scene of the shoot-out; only the women that are left to mourn the dead. Frances addresses the audience after reciting the victims' names, saying, "And I wish you had not thought to come here. And acted like it was something it was you needed to watch." This comment acknowledges that this is indeed a solemn space where trauma took place and that these women were the ones left to decide whether to tell the tale or not.[40] The silence is palpable in the audience and harrowing in the actual place where lives were lost. It is here that audience members participate in Blankenship's idea of rhetorical empathy as emotions are shared between Frances and the audience. Frances demands attention, and the audience is forced to give it to her. The "healing" of the play falls here as the audience feels not only pity but also empathy for her and everyone involved.

Levering gives Frances the last lines of the play. Her meaningful lines hinge on her experience. She is talking about the courthouse when she refers to "this place here where I never come and never will again." Her words resonate strongly because she was not at the courthouse during the shoot-out and did not even visit Hillsville after the shoot-out.[41] It was too traumatic for her. Claude and Floyd's funeral contribute to her trauma. She describes the people at the funeral as the "awfullest [*sic*] crowd you ever laid eyes on." She mentions that Claude's coffin was open. She then says, "[I] walked past Floyd and I never did, would not look at my husband. When I came to Claude, I cradled my boy. I cradled him in my arms. I cradled my cold baby. He was so cold for the longest time."[42] Through these statements, we see that her grief is tied to her motherhood. She does not look at Floyd because she is more concerned for Claude, whom she doted over his entire life. Giving her these lines, Levering offers a compassionate look at the shoot-out and the impact of the loss on her personally. She calls out the audience for being spectators and gawkers at this traumatic event. She hopes that we're satisfied in investing in the bloody story that left her with no husband or son. We indeed are left curious as to what draws us, as spectators, to want to learn more about the shoot-out and its aftermath. Unlike the display in the museum, we as audience members are made to feel pity through Frances's voice and experience.

Conclusion

The acknowledgment of the historical silence in archives and the recovered voices of these women through the play represent a new remembering of the shoot-out from the courthouse museum. While the male-centric, violent exhibits downstairs exist in glass and on peg board, Jezebel's refusal to talk about the shoot-out exposes just how traumatic the event was and the power that she holds over the narrative. Maude Iroler's actions led to the capture of J. Sidna Allen and Wesley Edwards, which initiated the end of the shoot-out saga. Despite this act, like Jezebel, she still wanted to remain silent because the event was too traumatic for her, even after distancing herself from the family by marrying another man. Meanwhile, Frances's letter demonstrates how truly dire her situation was when Floyd and Claude were incarcerated. In addition, Betty's decision to give the wrong picture to the detectives was a subtle act of deviance that helped lead the detectives away from her husband. Revealing these documents and actions show how each of these women did indeed have a part in the events of the shoot-out even if they occurred after the actual event. These actions are significant because they present another aspect of how these families were affected by the event.

The documents and actions create a new rhetorical remembering, and Levering's inclusion of Frances and Betty in his plays conveys a new empathetic remembering. While Levering and many other performance scholars state that the performance is temporary, its embodiment in the local gives it staying power. As Diana Taylor writes, the performance "evokes memories and grief that belong to some other body. It conjures up and makes visible not just the living but the powerful army of the always already living" in the courthouse.[43] Even Frances Allen in the last scene notes that the audience will think about the play as they "crawl into [their] beds and have [. . .] a safe dream."[44] Embodiment does not only stay on the stage though. It is also in the embodiment of the shoot-out's ancestors in the traumatic space that brings power and healing to the courthouse. The historic incident deemed unspeakable by those who witnessed it is now enacted and embraced by those buying tickets to see it. This embodiment certainly evokes Blankenship's idea of rhetorical empathy as it is "countering apathy and the paralysis of anger and cynicism. Rhetorical empathy [balances] and sustains. There is a place for both critique and repair."[45] In the case of the shoot-out plays, the traumatic anger caused by the historical event is counterbalanced by the empathetic portrayals of both sides. Audience and community members leave with a renewed remembering of the event. This change is so significant that often some of the actors in the play perform in roles that are the opposite of the side of their ancestors. The play stands as a powerful transformative act that helps heal a century-long traumatic fissure in the town of Hillsville. By the end of it, both actors and audience members are indeed "well satisfied" as they acknowledge what happened in the past and how that past plays in the present conditions of their own lives as they continue to heal from the tragedy.

Conclusion

Hillsville Remembered

They'll make a movie on this, this'll be as big as the Hatfields and McCoys ever dared to be.

It's been over 100 years, but people are still talking about what happened in the Carroll County courthouse that day. The echoes of the gun fire have long since disappeared, but the wounds left behind in this quaint little town of Hillsville have continued to fester. The political drama that led to the shooting has divided families for generations. Some say the shootout was self-defense, others murder. Many of the questions surrounding that day have yet to be answered.[1]

Chad Tucker, *57 Shots in 90 Seconds*

The preceding text is how the *57 Shots in 90 Seconds* podcast by Chad Tucker from Fox 8 News based in Greensboro, North Carolina, begins. Released in August 2020, this podcast is proof that even today, 109 years later, interest in the shoot-out is still evident and that rhetorical rememberings continue to be constructed about the event. In the three-episode podcast, Tucker recruits local Hillsville historians and community members to talk through the event. Coming after a few voices on the history of the shoot-out, the blurb about the connection to the Hatfields and McCoys demonstrates an immediate connection to Appalachian feuding and a Hollywood movie. This statement relates to the speculative rememberings from the media right after the shoot-out. Tucker shows the necessity of setting the shoot-out in the region of Appalachia through the trope of the feud—a common masculine-based, violent act. As a piece of recent journalism, however, the podcast attempts to present both sides of the shoot-out. By doing so, it creates empathetic rhetorics but does not come close to the empathy that the women characters in Levering's plays convey. The podcast first constructs the outlaw image (dramatized by music and sound effects) and then strives for empathy, but fails, much like many of the museum depictions. Through its existence, we can see how the shoot-out is still relevant, but we also see how the rhetorical rememberings of the previous chapters come together to form a new one that exists in the podcast, a new genre for the shoot-out.

While the media, like this podcast, continues to give stereotypical images from outside the region (the podcast is based in Greensboro, North Carolina), artistic performances of the shoot-out give us insider depictions of the shoot-out. These performances in the ballads and plays demonstrate the change from stereotypical rememberings to sympathetic ones. Participating in a historically Appalachian genre, the "Sidna Allen" ballad bifurcates the local government side and the Allen family side. The vicious, violent mountaineer presented in this ballad still resonates today in the minds of many citizens. In a recent trip to Hillsville, I found out that some of the tax money from the county was going toward the renovations of the historic J. Sidna Allen House. Consequently, there was upheaval in the town because many citizens did not want their hard-earned money to be spent on that project. However, "Claude Allen" presents a more sympathetic view of a young man who was merely defending his father. After his death, his mother and girlfriend weep at his grave, signifying Claude as a tragic hero. This ballad represents the start of the empathetic rhetoric that Levering's plays represent so well.

These plays add to the realistic trauma felt by those who suffered due to the shoot-out. The plays, performed on the historic site, gathered community members and descendants as they memorialized the shoot-out. Levering intentionally writes moments in the play that acknowledge its presence in the historic courthouse. These moments create empathetic rhetoric because they encourage the audience to negotiate their feelings about the shoot-out. They invite participation and make the audience remember that they are "greedy for guns and blood. You want to see folks shot, dead."[2] Through these plays, the past blurs with the present; the players depict the history quite literally as they lie on the floor, possibly in the same spot where the characters they play (and possibly their own ancestors) died, encouraging more emotion and empathy. Audience members are indeed not, as Frances Allen says at the end of the play, "well satisfied," but they are perhaps horrified by the depictions of the tragic event rendering the use of the tragic remembering. This reemergence of the trauma that was silenced for so long helps to reopen the conversation so that the community can talk to each other about the tragedy.

These plays would not be as powerful if they did not take place in the historic courthouse. The creation of these spaces of public memory demonstrates the vernacular and official retellings of the shoot-out. Like the media and artistic portrayals, these places and spaces convey different constructions of the shoot-out through different rhetorical rememberings. The historic courthouse museum conveys a vernacular retelling that creates epideictic history making as the curator Bill Webb talks through the shoot-out and exhibits. Besides his retelling of the story, the exhibits themselves tell a tale that focuses on J. Sidna Allen's reformation and the buildup to the shoot-out. It still depends on the outlaw image of the men, but the local exhibits give patrons a more humanistic portrayal of the family. In opposition, the Mount Airy Museum of Regional History conveys a broader construction of the shoot-out. It places Hillsville in the context of the Appalachian region, operating as an example of what can happen in a small mountain town during the Progressive

Era. This depiction is official because it is housed inside a government-funded museum. Despite the exhibit being less detailed than the other exhibits in the museum, it is still carefully organized; however, it, too, depends on stereotypical constructions of the Allens because of its dependence on the newspapers. Thus, while the "story of the century" is logically organized, it is still sensationalized in this exhibit. Outside of both of these constructions is the Harmon Museum. Solely based on vernacular storytelling, this museum relies on a smattering of artifacts that Harmon collected. Patrons must spend time walking down the aisles to decipher the construction of the shoot-out through newspaper articles, framed pictures, and other material artifacts. It depends totally on the images of the violent mountaineer through the use of the newspapers. Clearly, the sheer number of museums about the event in this small town indicates that the local citizens believe that this is an event worth remembering in several different ways.

Until the recent Levering plays, silence played a large role in the women's roles in the shoot-out. Frances Allen, Betty Allen, Jezebel Goad, and Maude Iroler all participated in rhetorical actions that impacted the shoot-out and its aftermath. They continued their lives after the shoot-out and had to put their families back together. Intentionally engaging in silence, they proved themselves resilient mountain women who survived this tragic event. The fictional characters of Levering's plays demonstrate that there is not only a desire to hear these voices recovered, but also an empathetic way to convey healing for the town. The characters' portrayals offer a way for both sides of the town to come together and remember the event.

These constructions of Hillsville, however, do not stay within the confines of the town. In each construction, we see how Hillsville represents Appalachia. Seen in the contemporary depictions of Levering's plays and in the continual interest in the event by independent scholars, such as local community member Howard Sadler, who presented on finding the affidavit served to Floyd Allen, the event is still very much on the minds of the town's citizens. In fact, in the spring of 2022, there will be a ceremony for the return of this document from the Wytheville courts to its home in Hillsville. Implicit in these performances or not, these actions and retellings depict Hillsville as a mountain community in Appalachia. The local retellings of the event fight against modern depictions of the region. One such moment is when Kay Cox as Betty Allen refers to her own death in the papers. This spectacular moment in the play prompts laughter in the audience because it shows how the media coverage of the shoot-out is a farce. The production of these cultural performances replaces the popular stereotypical and, quite frankly, harmful rhetorics that are produced today in television shows and in popular nonfiction written about the region.

Similar to the media accounts about the shoot-out and histories, popular depictions of the hillbilly figure still portray Appalachia as a forgotten or lost region whose people are backward. Since J. W. Williamson published *Hillbillyland: What the Movies Did to the Mountains and What the Mountains Did to the Movies* (1995) and Emily Satterwhite's *Dear Appalachia: Readers, Identity, and Popular Fiction Since 1878* (2015), we continue to see how there is a consistent depiction of Appalachia as a stereotyped, exploited region in popular culture. These depictions directly echo those rendered in the violent mountaineer and uncivilized other rhetorical rememberings seen in the media coverage of Hillsville. For example, *Appalachian Outlaws* (2014–2015), a popular show on the History Channel, participates in this pioneer imagery of Appalachia on its website, which says,

> As the rest of the United States has evolved through time, the Appalachians have stood the test of it. For centuries, its mountainous landscape has acted as a cultural barrier to the influences of the outside world, and its inhabitants act more like their ancestors from the 1700s than their modern-day peers.[3]

Similar to the ethnic grounding in the early media portrayals of the shoot-out, these depictions present Appalachia as a cultural oasis, a land whose people "act more like their ancestors from the 1700s than their modern-day peers." These images relate directly to the ethnic images of the Allen men, who only knew the mountains and their own "clan." Clan imagery in Appalachia also operates in the show *Outsiders* (2016–2017) where, like *Appalachian Outlaws*, the members of the mountain town restrict themselves to their Kentucky hollers to attempt to live off the grid. They defend their right to live in the mountains just as their ancestors did, and those who come to threaten them and their way of life face consequences. Grounded in masculinity and violence, the show again perpetuates the stereotypes that the media created about the shoot-out in the early twentieth century.

While *Appalachian Outlaws* and *Outsiders* depict a rejection of modern society in Appalachia, the television show *Justified* (2010–2015) attempts to modernize the region. Based in Harlan and Lexington, Kentucky, protagonist Raylan Givens has to negotiate being a U.S. marshal in a town where he is kin to or friends with local lawbreakers. The show addresses contemporary issues like religion, drugs, and mountaintop removal. Much like the depictions of the Allens in the plays and some of the museums, Raylan is a realistic character who has his own flaws but attempts to stand for justice and his own morals. He, like the Allens, sometimes shoots first and asks questions later. Like the mass media frenzy right after the shoot-out, these shows present constructions of Appalachia for the American public.

Similar to the change we see as we go from the stereotypical "Sidna Allen" ballad to the empathy of the "Claude Allen" ballad and Levering's plays, current documentaries and series now cast a sympathetic and brutally honest depiction of the region. *Hillbilly* (2018), a documentary directed by Sally Rubin and Ashley York and written by both along with Appalachian writer Silas House, includes various voices from inside the region to explain the political and economic complexities of Appalachia. *Dopesick* (2021) is a series that takes place in Appalachia and shows the devastation of oxytocin and opioid abuse in the region. It's depiction of Appalachia's addiction crisis is harrowing. The uprising of the affected communities does, however, show the determination and empathy of these Appalachian communities.

In opposition to these depictions, the most popular presentation of the region still engaging with these rhetorical rememberings is found in J. D. Vance's *New York Times* bestselling book, *Hillbilly Elegy: A Memoir of a Family and Culture in Crisis* (2016). In this text and the new Netflix film (2020), Vance and director Ron Howard present an Appalachia that is wasted with drug abuse, violence, and poverty. Similar to the early fictional novels of the shoot-out, Vance depends on violence to weave his personal narrative. His story begins sympathetically as he recounts his childhood and the violent nature of his family members; however, these characteristics rely on hyperbole and exaggeration. Similar to *Dancing Outlaw* (1991), *The Wild and Wonderful Whites of West Virginia* (2009), and *Deliverance* (1972), his narrative depends on speculation and specter instead of reality. Unlike the more recent documentaries and shows, Vance's descriptions of Appalachia are created to make money and *not* tell a story of a realistic Appalachia. Through his own experience, he argues that Appalachia can help itself just as he did as he ascended into a new socioeconomic class and became a lawyer. He rejects any of the systematic oppression that happens in the Appalachian region and instead uses his voice and experience to speak for all of Appalachia. He engages with the same stereotypes of Appalachia as an uncivilized other that the media presented right after the shoot-out. His Appalachia is filled with a culture that remains in the past, refusing to look toward the future.

However, there is a pushback of this written Appalachia through texts like *Appalachian Reckoning: A Region Responds to*

Courthouse with Love, Hillsville, VA. Photograph by author.

Hillbilly Elegy and *What You Are Getting Wrong about Appalachia.* Similar to the development of the shoot-out, there is also a profound turn to the feminine narrative, as seen in *Hill Women: Finding Family and a Way Forward in the Appalachian Mountains*. Western North Carolina writer Leah Hampton notes that "we have eluded rural women for profit and personal advancement far too long. Only by re-focusing and re-centering on our dominant feminine and non-binary folkways can this country begin to heal itself."[4] While this statement about the country is hyperbolic, I would argue that these new approaches to raising women's voices not only brings a new narrative to the rememberings of the shoot-out but also encourages a more empathetic view that encourages healing for the town. Seen in Fig. 6.1, the word *love* appears outside the courthouse. These words appear as a tourism promotion for the state of Virginia, but I find this image to be a wonderful metaphor for the mending of the town after decades of hard feelings.

Seen through these examples, the courthouse shoot-out in Hillsville stands as an important part of our culture today because it symbolizes how Appalachia continues to be rhetorically constructed by those inside and outside the region. Perhaps research about the event will never be able to "see through the smoke" to reveal a true Appalachia nor a true Hillsville, but depictions like Levering's plays work against still recent stereotypes that are derogatory, exploitative, and harmful to the region. They encourage an empathetic remembering that involves healing on both sides of the shoot-out. The true tragedy of the shoot-out lies not in the depictions that outsiders made of those involved nor in its bloody history, but in our inability to understand how this historic event can have a remarkable presence in our past, present, and future.

Acknowledgments

This project would not have happened without the participation of my contacts in Hillsville, Virginia, who took time out of their lives to talk with me about the shoot-out. My most sincere appreciation goes to Bill Webb, Gary Marshall, Kay Cox, Howard Sadler, Allison Craig, and Ronald W. Hall. May this text bring a new perspective to an event that has had more impact on each of your lives than I could articulate within this study.

I'd like to express my thanks to the Department of English Studies at Western Carolina University, particularly to Brent Kinser, who served as the department head and my mentor through this project. All my colleagues there have been incredibly supportive of this project, and I'm grateful to work with such wonderful, compassionate folks. I'd like to also extend thanks to the Western Carolina University College of Arts and Sciences for supporting my work and scholarship.

I want to thank each person who worked with me on this project. This project started in John Williams's last section of Appalachian History Seminar at Appalachian State University. A new and expanded version of that project turned into my dissertation, so I'd like to thank my dissertation committee: Sara Webb-Sunderhaus, Tim Johnson, Amy Clukey, and my director, Stephen Schneider. Thanks to each of you for your support during that process. This manuscript is better for your input.

I could not have done this project without my friends and colleagues who read several drafts of it and supported me through the process. Jonathan Bradshaw and Erin Zimmerman looked at several drafts of the dissertation and have been loyal friends for many years.

To my bestie, Deanna Laur, thank you for your unwavering support and encouragement from when I first started this in Boone, North Carolina, to this publication.

To my friends and mentors who helped me along this journey: Georgia Rhoades and Dennis Bohr, Jean W. Cash, Geoffrey and Sarah Hirsh, Sam and Rachel Bartlett, Deborah Hopkins, Lilly Knoepp, Bryan Miler, Brian and Kiley Brodeur, Jessika Griffin, Michael and Sarah Boatright, Kathy Schenk, Keri Kepps, Emily and LB Brier, Suzanne Stone, and many others who have listened and contributed to the development and writing of this project.

My editor, Patrick D. O'Dowd, has been patient through the entire process and continued to believe in me. I'm so grateful for your encouragement, tenacity, and overall kindness. Thank you, and I look forward to working with you and University of Kentucky Press more in the future.

I want to thank my parents, Alan and Cheryl Rountree, and my sister and brother-in-law, Molly and Justin Trask, for their unwavering support through not only this project, but also my educational career as a whole. Their continued encouragement helped me to realize my full potential as an academic. We may not have it all together, but together we have it all. Love y'all.

Finally, to Caleb Pendygraft, who has been with me not only through this writing process, but also through the dissertation from which it grew. I owe you the deepest heartfelt thanks. Always.

Notes

Introduction

1. Frank Levering, *Thunder in the Hills,* Hillsville, VA, March 24 and 25, 2012. Personal copy.

2. Ronald W. Hall, *The Carroll County Courthouse Tragedy: A True Account of the 1912 Gun Battle That Shocked the Nation; Its Causes and the Aftermath* (Second Reprinting. Hillsville, VA: The Carroll County Historical Society, 2003), 45.

3. Hall, *The Carroll County Courthouse Tragedy*, 52.

4. Randal L. Hall, "Constructing Violence: Historical Memory and a 1912 Courtroom Massacre in Virginia's Blue Ridge Mountains," in *(Re) Constructing Cultures of Violence and Peace*, ed. Richard Jackson (New York: Rodopi, 2004), 3.

5. Hall, "Constructing Violence," 268.

6. Phillip J. Obermiller and Shaunna L. Scott, "Making Appalachia: Interdisciplinary Fields and Appalachian Studies," in *Studying Appalachian Studies, Making the Path by Walking*, eds. Chad Berry, Phillip J. Obermiller, and Shaunna L. Scott (Urbana: University of Illinois Press, 2015), 145.

7. Adam H. Domby, *The False Cause: Fraud, Fabrication, and White Supremacy in Confederate Memory* (Charlottesville: University of Virginia Press, 2020), 6.

8. Greg Dickinson, Carole Blair, and Brian L. Ott, eds., *Places of Public Memory: The Rhetoric of Museums and Memorials*. Rhetoric, Culture, and Social Critique (Tuscaloosa: University of Alabama Press, 2010), 6.

9. Dickinson, Blair, and Ott, *Places of Public Memory*, 7.

10. Ibid.

11. Ibid., 13.

12. John E. Bodnar, *Remaking America: Public Memory, Commemoration, and Patriotism in the Twentieth Century* (Princeton, NJ: Princeton University Press, 1992), 13.

13. Ibid., 14.

14. Ibid.

15. Jim Ridolfo and Danielle Nicole DeVoss, "Composing for Recomposition: Rhetorical Velocity and Delivery," *Kairos* 13, no. 2 (January 15, 2009).

16. Lisa Blankenship, *Changing the Subject: A Theory of Rhetorical Empathy* (Logan: Utah State University Press, 2019), 7.

17. Blankenship, *Changing the Subject*, 7.

1. "The Many Untruths"

1. Betsy W. Chandler, *Memoirs of J. Sidna Allen: A True Narrative of What Really Happened at Hillsville, Virginia* (Eden, NC: Alwith Publishing, 1929), 88.

2. Ronald W. Hall, *The Carroll County Courthouse Tragedy: A True Account of the 1912 Gun Battle That Shocked the Nation; Its Causes and the Aftermath* (Second Reprinting. Hillsville, VA: The Carroll County Historical Society, 2003), 78–79.

3. "Expecting Death in Discharge of Their Duty, Court Officers Are Shot Down in Cold Blood by Carroll County Desperados," *Richmond Times-Dispatch*, March 15, 1912, 18, 923 edition.

4. "Mob Wipe Out Court," *Kansas Baptist Herald*, March 16, 1912, n.p.

5. "Outlaws Slay Judge in Court," *New York Times*, March 18, 1912, 1.

6. Henry D. Shapiro, *Appalachia on Our Mind: The Southern Mountains and Mountaineers in the American Consciousness, 1870–1920* (Chapel Hill: University of North Carolina Press, 1978), 44.

7. Michael E. McGerr, *A Fierce Discontent: The Rise and Fall of the Progressive Movement in America, 1870–1920* (Oxford: Oxford UP, 2005), xiv.

8. Ibid.

9. Ronald L. Lewis, *The Industrialist and the Mountaineer: The Eastham-Thompson Feud and the Struggle for West Virginia's Timber Frontier* (Morgantown: West Virginia UP, 2017), 6; quotation from David Thelan, *Paths of Resistance: Tradition and Dignity in Industrializing Missouri*, 45–46.

10. Randal L. Hall, "Constructing Violence: Historical Memory and a 1912 Courtroom Massacre in Virginia's Blue Ridge Mountains," in *(Re)*

Constructing Cultures of Violence and Peace, ed. Richard Jackson (New York: Rodopi, 2004), 32.

11. Later in the twentieth century, historians further added academic stereotyping to the region that the fiction writers create. Works such as Horace Kephart's *Our Southern Highlanders* (1913), John C. Campbell's *The Southern Highlander and His Homeland* (1921), Jack Weller's *Yesterday's People* (1965), or Henry Shapiro's *Appalachia on Our Mind* (1978) contribute to exceptionalism ideas of Appalachia, much like the identification of the lowland South at the time. These writers describe mountaineers as "yesterday's people," designating the mountain culture as a thing of the past. Oftentimes, these writers recognized Appalachia as an uncivilized other to be examined as through a microscope. Mountain society and customs interested these historians to the point that they declared it was a region worth studying because of its distinct features.

12. Allen Batteau, *The Invention of Appalachia* (The Anthropology of Form and Meaning) (Tucson, AZ: University of Arizona Press, 1990), 88.

13. Ibid.

14. John Alexander Williams, *Appalachia: A History* (Chapel Hill: University of North Carolina Press, 2002), 186.

15. T. R. C. Hutton, *Bloody Breathitt: Politics and Violence in the Appalachian South* (Lexington: University of Kentucky Press, 2015), 1.

16. Ibid., 55

17. Altina L. Waller, *Feud: Hatfields, McCoys, and Social Change in Appalachia, 1860–1900* (Chapel Hill: University of North Carolina Press, 1988), 209.

18. Ibid., 210.

19. *New York Times* qtd. in Altina L. Waller, *Feud: Hatfields, McCoys, and Social Change in Appalachia, 1860–1900* (Chapel Hill: University of North Carolina Press, 1988), 214.

20. Hall, *The Carroll County Courthouse Tragedy*, 137.

21. Ibid., 134.

22. "The Recall at Hillsville," *New York Times*, March 15, 1912, 9.

23. Ibid.

24. "Three Killed in Virginia Court: Allen's Gang Illustrates the Recall by Murdering the Judge, Sheriff and Prosecutor," *Wall Street Journal*. March 15, 1912, 6.

25. Ibid., author emphasis.

26. "Two More Dead in Allen Feud," *New York Times*, March 16, 1912, 1.

27. "Dead Judge Was Fine Shot: Thorton Massie a Man of Iron Nerve and Great Strength," *New York Times*, March 16, 1912, 1.

28. "Mob Wipe Out Court," *Kansas Baptist Herald*, March 16, 1912, n.p.

29. Ibid.

30. Ibid.

31. Ibid.

32. Anthony Harkins, *Hillbilly: A Cultural History of an American Icon* (Oxford: Oxford UP, 2004), 61.

33. "Explanations That Are Excuses," *New York Times*, March 25, 1912, 6.

34. "Outlaws Slay Judge in Court," *New York Times*, March 18, 1912, 1.

35. Ibid.

36. Ibid.

37. Ibid.

38. "Outlaw Once an Officer," *New York Times*, March 17, 1912, 6.

39. Ibid.

40. "Shoot the Judge," *Wall Street Journal*, March 18, 1912, 6.

41. Harkins, *Hillbilly*, 35.

42. Ibid, 36.

43. "Of Course They Are Not Monsters," *New York Times*, March 22, 1912, 8.

44. Ibid.

45. Ibid.

46. "Should Be a Hunt, Not a War," *New York Times*, March 19, 1912, sec. Voices of the Times. ProQuest Historical Newspapers. The New York Times, 10.

47. Ibid.

48. Ibid.

49. "Highways and Byways: The People's Rule in Government," *The Chautauquan: A Weekly Newsmagazine*, June 1912. American Periodicals.

50. Floyd Allen, "Statement," (Accession 28355. Personal Papers Collection, The Library of Virginia. Richmond, VA, March 29, 1913).

51. "Allens Executed: Respite Plan Failed," *New York Times*, March 29, 1912, 11.

52. Ibid.

53. Chandler, *Memoirs of J. Sidna Allen*, 117.

54. Ibid., 66.

55. Ibid.

56. Ibid.

57. Harkins, *Hillbilly*, 66.

58. Ibid.

59. Ibid.

60. This duality is also reminiscent of how citizens embrace the shoot-out currently. They're proud that it draws tourists in, but feelings are also still raw about the event.

61. "Obsessions Should Be Shunned," *New York Times*, April 24, 1912, 6.

62. Ibid.

63. Frank Levering, *Thunder in the Hills,* Hillsville, VA, March 24 and 25, 2012. Personal copy.

2. Performing Hillsville, Part One

1. Rebecca Schneider, *Performing Remains: Art and War in Times of Theatrical Reenactment* (Abingdon, Oxon; New York: Routledge, 2011), 101.

2. "Tom Dooley" is a murder ballad that explains the murder and trial of Tom Dooley, whom the state of North Carolina accused of murdering his girlfriend, Laurie Foster. He was hung in Asheville, North Carolina, for her murder. The trial continues to be a piece of local folklore in the region through the ballad and stories that surround it.

3. Roger DeV Renwick, "Ballad," in *American Folklore*, ed. Jan Harold Brunvand, third edition (New York: Garland, 1996), 57, 57–61.

4. Ibid.

5. Barre Toelken, "Ballads and Folksongs," in *Folk Groups and Folklore Genres: An Introduction*, ed. Elliot Oring (Logan: Utah State University Press, 1986), 152, 147–74.

6. "Talk at the G.F. Women's Club Asheville, NC" 6 June 1957, Isaac Garfield Greer Papers, Audio Files Series, W. L. Eury Appalachian Collection, Appalachian State U, Boone, NC. This description is taken from a recording that I received from I. G. Greer from the I. G. Greer Folksong Collection at Appalachian State University's Belk Library and Information Commons. The recording was on a wax cylinder and was converted to CD for me by one of the archivists there. I never had the privilege of knowing Professor Greer, who passed away in 1967; however, I did have his great-grandson in my Appalachian Studies course at Caldwell Community College, where I played

this clip for him. It was the first time he had heard his great-grandfather's voice. I use this anecdote to illustrate just how powerful the study of ballads and ballad collecting still remains in the twenty-first century.

7. Renwick, "Ballad," 60.

8. Ibid., 58.

9. Diana Taylor, *The Archive and the Repertoire: Performing Cultural Memory in the Americas* (Durham: Duke University Press, 2003), 19.

10. Edward S. Casey and Kendall R. Phillips, "'Public Memory in Place and Time,'" in *Framing Public Memory* (Tuscaloosa: University of Alabama Press, 2004), 23, 17–44.

11. Greg Dickinson, Carole Blair, and Brian L. Ott, eds., "Rhetoric, Culture, and Social Critique," in *Places of Public Memory: The Rhetoric of Museums and Memorials*. (Tuscaloosa: University of Alabama Press, 2010), 6.

12. Ibid.

13. Ivan Tribe, *An Appalachian Family and the Music That Shaped Their Lives* (Urbana-Champagne: University of Illinois Press, 1993), 69.

14. Peter Aceves, "The Hillsville Tragedy in Court Record, Mass Media and Folk Balladry: A Problem in Historical Documentation," *Keystone Folklore Quarterly*, Spring issue (1971): 1–38, 10.

15. Ibid.

16. Ibid., 25.

17. Ibid., 11.

18. Ronald W. Hall, *The Carroll County Courthouse Tragedy: A True Account of the 1912 Gun Battle That Shocked the Nation; Its Causes and the Aftermath* (Second Reprinting. Hillsville, VA: The Carroll County Historical Society, 2003), 26.

19. "Outlaw Once an Officer," *New York Times*, March 17, 1912, 6.

20. Ibid.

21. Hall, *The Carroll County Courthouse Tragedy*, 214, 255.

22. "Sidney" is the mountain vernacular term for "Sidna." Ballad variations appear under both names.

23. Aceves, "The Hillsville Tragedy in Court Record, Mass Media, and Folk Balladry," 28.

24. Ibid.

25. Ibid.

26. Ibid., 27.

27. Ibid.

28. Ibid., 28.

29. Ibid., 29.

30. Ibid.

31. Ibid., 34.

32. Hall, *The Carroll County Courthouse Tragedy*, 22.

33. Betsy W. Chandler, *Memoirs of J. Sidna Allen: A True Narrative of What Really Happened at Hillsville, Virginia* (Eden, NC: Alwith Publishing, 1929), 108.

34. Ibid., 109.

35. Hall, *The Carroll County Courthouse Tragedy*, 238.

36. Victor Allen, Personal Interview July 9, 2016.

37. Aceves, "The Hillsville Tragedy in Court Record," 19.

38. Ibid.

39. Ibid., 21.

40. Ibid., 19.

41. Ibid.

42. Ibid., 20.

43. Ibid.

44. Ibid., 21.

45. Ibid., 24.

46. Ibid., 23.

47. Ibid., 18.

48. There is a long line of contemporary musical compositions based on or around the shoot-out, including a rock opera titled "Sid Allen and the Devil's Den" by Tom Harvey and acoustic songs written by local musicians, such as John Carpenter's song from the perspectives of family members and Philip W. Jones's "Floyd's Lament," but the local ballads serve as ground zero for the rest of these musical renditions to develop.

49. Ibid.

3. Performing Hillsville, Part Two

1. Frank Levering, *Thunder in the Hills*, Hillsville, VA, March 24 and 25, 2012. Personal copy.

2. John Smith, "Trauma," in *Keywords for Southern Studies*, eds. Scott Romine and Jennifer Rae Greeson (Athens: University of Georgia Press, 2016), 354–65.

3. Tom Bowers, "The Ethics of Memory: Commemorating Disasters in an Age of Risk," *Southern Communication Journal* 80, no. 2 (2015): 119–36, 119.

4. After being told about the plays, I wanted to see them or read the script. One of my informants was able to give me a DVD of the plays that he recorded during one of the productions. He specifically told me not to make copies and that I was only to use it for this project. While I would like to gain access to all of the plays at a certain point, this production seems most relevant to analyze because of its use at the centennial, its expanded length, and mostly because this play recognizes its status as a cultural artifact that represents the shoot-out.

5. Levering, *Thunder in the Hills*, 2012.

6. Ibid.

7. Bill Webb, interview with the author, July 8, 2016.

8. Ronald W. Hall, *The Carroll County Courthouse Tragedy: A True Account of the 1912 Gun Battle That Shocked the Nation; Its Causes and the Aftermath* (Second Reprinting. Hillsville, VA: The Carroll County Historical Society, 2003), 238.

9. Ibid., 239.

10. Levering, *Thunder in the Hills*, 2012.

11. Victor Allen, interview with the author, July 9, 2016.

12. Levering, *Thunder in the Hills*, 2012.

13. Diana Taylor, *The Archive and the Repertoire: Performing Cultural Memory in the Americas* (Durham: Duke University Press, 2003), 188 (her emphasis).

14. Rebecca Schneider, *Performing Remains: Art and War in Times of Theatrical Reenactment* (Abingdon, Oxon; New York: Routledge, 2011), 104.

15. Ibid.

16. Ibid. (author's emphasis)

17. Taylor, *The Archive and the Repertoire*, 143.

18. Ibid.

19. Wendy S. Hesford, *Spectacular Rhetorics: Human Rights Visions, Recognitions, Feminisms* Next Wave (Durham, NC: Duke University Press, 2011), 8.

20. Ibid., 17.

21. Levering, *Thunder in the Hills*, 2012.

22. Many locals in Hillsville still continue to collect artifacts from the shootout from newspaper clippings to the badge that was given to Claude Allen after his death. Chapter Three will explain more about how these archival sites are important in the circulation of the history of the event.

23. Schneider, *Performing Remains.*, 15.

24. Levering, *Thunder in the Hills*, 2012.

25. Ibid.

26. Ibid.

27. Ibid.

28. Taylor, *The Archive and the Repertoire*, 143.

29. Levering, *Thunder in the Hills*, 2012.

30. Ibid.

31. Ibid.

32. Ibid.

33. Ibid.

34. Ibid.

35. Ibid.

36. Ibid.

37. Ibid.

38. Ibid.

39. Ibid.

40. Ibid.

41. Ibid.

42. Ibid.

43. Schneider, *Performing Remains*, 104.

44. Taylor, *The Archive and the Repertoire.*, 143.

45. Ibid.

4. "Feelings Are Still Very Strong"

1. In addition to the money from the plays, there have been *several* other attempts to raise funds for the renovations to the J. Sidna Allen House and to circulate the perceptions of this place of public memory. One is the work of Rita Edlein, who took nostalgic pictures of the house with her subjects posing provocatively around it. These pictures were made into cards and sold at the courthouse museum. Volunteers at the museum told me that the art wasn't their style but that some visitors liked the contemporary take

on the old building. In addition to the cards, the museum sells Christmas ornaments to fund the renovation. There is also a Friends of J. Sidna Allen House Facebook group to keep those online aware of the fundraising and renovations of the house.

2. John E. Bodnar, *Remaking America: Public Memory, Commemoration, and Patriotism in the Twentieth Century* (Princeton, NJ: Princeton University Press, 1992), 14.

3. Cynthia Miecznkowski Sheard, "The Public Value of Epideictic Rhetoric," *College English* 58, no. 7 (November 1996): 765–94, 771.

4. Greg Dickinson, Carole Blair, and Brian L. Ott, eds., *Places of Public Memory: The Rhetoric of Museums and Memorials*. Rhetoric, Culture, and Social Critique (Tuscaloosa: University of Alabama Press, 2010), 26.

5. Ibid., 29.

6. All of the displays are explained on regular paper. These displays demonstrate how, despite low budgetary concerns, the shoot-out still remains an important part of Hillsville history.

7. The inscription reads, "Sacred to the Memory of Claude S. Allen and his father who was judicially murdered in the Va. Penitentiary March 28, 1913 by order of the Governer of the State over the protest of 100000 Citizens of the State of Va. Placed here by a friend and citizen of Va."

8. Bill Webb, interview with the author, 2016.

9. Mount Airy Museum of Regional History, "History," n.d. https://www.northcarolinamuseum.org/index.php?option=com_content&view=article&id=56&Itemid=79.

10. Donations can be made at their website as well, which could explain the amount of money poured into this museum as opposed to the Hillsville Museum.

11. The residents who support the Allen side call the shoot-out a "tragedy," whereas the residents who support the local government call it a "massacre."

12. Selling goods was how J. Sidna Allen made most of his money to afford to build his beautiful Victorian home.

13. Ronald W. Hall, *The Carroll County Courthouse Tragedy: A True Account of the 1912 Gun Battle That Shocked the Nation; Its Causes and the Aftermath* (Second Reprinting. Hillsville, VA: The Carroll County Historical Society, 2003), 257.

14. Bodnar, *Remaking America*, 14.

5. "I Wish You Had Not Thought to Come Here"

1. Lisa Blankenship, *Changing the Subject: A Theory of Rhetorical Empathy* (Logan: Utah State University Press, 2019), 17.

2. "Two More Dead in Allen Feud," *New York Times*, March 16, 1912.

3. Cheryl Glenn, and Jessica Enoch, "Invigorating Historiographic Practices in Rhetoric and Composition Studies," in *Working in the Archives, Practical Research Methods for Rhetoric and Composition*, eds. Alexis E. Ramsey, Wendy B. Sharer, Barbara L'Eplattenier, and Lisa S. Mastrangelo (Carbondale: Southern Illinois University Press, 2010), 23, 11–27.

4. Blankenship, *Changing the Subject*, 16.

5. Allen, "Statement."

6. Etta Donnan Mann, *Four Years in the Governor's Mansion of Virginia* (Richmond, VA: The Dietz Press, 1937), 99.

7. William "Bill" Lord, *The Red Ear of Corn* (Pittsburg, PA: Tri-Ad Litho, Inc., 1999), 107.

8. Kelley Ewing, "Jezebel Goad: Heroine of Hillsville," *The Uncommonwealth: Voices from the Library of Virginia* (blog), March 23, 2012. https://uncommonwealth.virginiamemory.com/blog/2012/03/23/jezebel-goad-heroine-of-hillsville/.

9. Jezebel Goad, "Letter," (TS, Floyd Landreth Papers Collection, The Library of Virginia. Richmond, VA, May 3, 1965).

10. Cheryl Glenn, *Unspoken: A Rhetoric of Silence* (Carbondale: Southern Illinois University Press, 2004), 23.

11. Ibid., 41.

12. Kay Cox, interview with the author, July 8, 2016.

13. "Two More Dead In Allen Feud."

14. J. Sidna Allen also describes this same fictional shoot-out in his memoir, but instead of referring to the newspaper articles, he remarks that the standoff at his house is written in a book.

15. Anita Puckett, "Aftermath of the Courthouse Tragedy," presented at the Courthouse Tragedy Centennial Symposium., Hillsville, VA, March 13, 2012.

16. Ibid.

17. Allen, "Statement."

18. Puckett states that in mid-December *the Richmond Evening Journal* had begun a fund to help Claude. This fund could have been attributed to Frances's letter to the *Galax Post Herald*.

19. Allen, "Statement."

20. Betsy W. Chandler, *Memoirs of J. Sidna Allen: A True Narrative of What Really Happened at Hillsville, Virginia* (Eden, NC: Alwith Publishing, 1929), 81.

21. Ibid, 83

22. "Catch Sidna Allen by Trailing Girl," *New York Times*, September 15, 1912, 6.

23. "Allen Explains Shootout." *New York Times* 16 Sept. 1912: 13:4.

24. "Catch Sidna Allen by Trailing Girl," *New York Times*, September 15, 1912, 6.

25. Ronald W. Hall, *The Carroll County Courthouse Tragedy: A True Account of the 1912 Gun Battle That Shocked the Nation; Its Causes and the Aftermath* (Second Reprinting. Hillsville, VA: The Carroll County Historical Society, 2003), 258.

26. Blankenship, *Changing the Subject*, 5.

27. Ibid.

28. Blankenship, *Changing the Subject*, 16.

29. Frank Levering, *Thunder in the Hills,* Hillsville, VA, March 24 and 25, 2012. Personal copy.

30. Ibid.

31. Ibid.

32. Ibid.

33. Ibid.

34. Ibid.

35. Levering does include a brief emotional breakdown of Floyd right before his electrocution, but it is most certainly *not* as emotional as Frances's before the performed shoot-out.

36. Levering, *Thunder in the Hills,* 2012.

37. Ibid.

38. Ibid.

39. Ibid.

40. Ibid.

41. Ibid.

42. Ibid.

43. Diana Taylor, *The Archive and the Repertoire: Performing Cultural Memory in the Americas* (Durham: Duke University Press, 2003), 143.

44. Levering, *Thunder in the Hills*, 2012.

45. Blankenship, *Changing the Subject*, 17.

Conclusion

1. Chad Tucker, "57 Shots in 90 Seconds," *57 Shots in 90 Seconds*, n.d. Accessed January 1, 2021.

2. Frank Levering, *Thunder in the Hills*, Hillsville, VA, March 24 and 25, 2012. Personal copy.

3. A&E Television Networks, "About Appalachian Outlaws," 2017.

4. Leah Hampton, "Lost in a (Mis)Gendered Appalachia," *Guernica* (blog), November 23, 2020.

Bibliography

Aceves, Peter. "The Hillsville Tragedy in Court Record, Mass Media and Folk Balladry: A Problem in Historical Documentation." *Keystone Folklore Quarterly*, Spring Issue (1971): 1–38.

The History Channel. *About Appalachian Outlaws*, July 1, 2017. https://www.history.com/shows/appalachian-outlaws.

"Allen Explains Shootout." *New York Times* (September 16, 1912), section 13.

Allen, Floyd. "Statement." Accession 28355. Personal Papers Collection, The Library of Virginia. Richmond, VA, March 29, 1913.

Allen, Victor. Interview with the author, July 9, 2016.

"Allens Executed: Respite Plan Failed." *New York Times* (March 29, 1912), 11.

Batteau, Allen. *The Invention of Appalachia*. The Anthropology of Form and Meaning. Tucson, AZ: University of Arizona Press, 1990.

Blankenship, Lisa. *Changing the Subject: A Theory of Rhetorical Empathy*. Logan: Utah State University Press, 2019.

Bodnar, John E. *Remaking America: Public Memory, Commemoration, and Patriotism in the Twentieth Century*. Princeton, NJ: Princeton University Press, 1992.

Bowers, Tom. "The Ethics of Memory: Commemorating Disasters in an Age of Risk." *Southern Communication Journal* 80, no. 2 (2015): 119–36.

Casey, Edward S., and Kendall R. Phillips. "Public Memory in Place and Time." In *Framing Public Memory*, edited by Kendall R. Phillips, 17–44. Tuscaloosa: University of Alabama Press, 2004.

"Catch Sidna Allen by Trailing Girl." *New York Times* (September 15, 1912) 1.

Catte, Elizabeth. *What You Are Getting Wrong about Appalachia*. First edition. Cleveland, Ohio: Belt Publishing, 2018.

Chandler, Betsy W. *Memoirs of J. Sidna Allen, A True Narrative of What Really Happened at Hillsville 1912*. Eden, NC: Alwith Publishing, 1929.

Bibliography

"Dead Judge Was Fine Shot: Thorton Massie a Man of Iron Nerve and Great Strength." *New York Times* (March 16, 1912), 1.

Dickinson, Greg, Carole Blair, and Brian L. Ott, eds. "Rhetoric, Culture, and Social Critique." In *Places of Public Memory: The Rhetoric of Museums and Memorials*. Tuscaloosa: University of Alabama Press, 2010.

Ewing, Kelley. "Jezebel Goad: Heroine of Hillsville." *The Uncommonwealth: Voices from the Library of Virginia* (blog), March 23, 2012. https://uncommonwealth.virginiamemory.com/blog/2012/03/23/jezebel-goad-heroine-of-hillsville/.

"Expecting Death in Discharge of Their Duty, Court Officers Are Shot Down in Cold Blood by Carroll County Desperados." *Richmond Times-Dispatch* (March 15, 1912), 18, 923 editions.

"Explanations That Are Excuses." *New York Times* (March 25, 1912), 6.

Glenn, Cheryl. *Unspoken: A Rhetoric of Silence*. Carbondale: Southern Illinois University Press, 2004.

Glenn, Cheryl, and Jessica Enoch. "Invigorating Historiographic Practices in Rhetoric and Composition Studies." In *Working in the Archives, Practical Research Methods for Rhetoric and Composition*, edited by Alexis E. Ramsey, Wendy B. Sharer, Barbara L'Eplattenier, and Lisa S. Mastrangelo, 11–27. Carbondale: Southern Illinois University Press, 2010.

Goad, Jezebel. "Letter." TS. Floyd Landreth Papers Collection, The Library of Virginia. Richmond, VA, May 3, 1965.

Hall, Randal L. "Constructing Violence: Historical Memory and a 1912 Courtroom Massacre in Virginia's Blue Ridge Mountains." In *(Re) Constructing Cultures of Violence and Peace*, edited by Richard Jackson, 26. New York: Rodopi, 2004.

Hall, Ronald W. *The Carroll County Courthouse Tragedy: A True Account of the 1912 Gun Battle That Shocked the Nation; Its Causes and the Aftermath*. Second Reprinting. Hillsville, VA: The Carroll County Historical Society, 2003.

Hampton, Leah. "Lost in a (Mis)Gendered Appalachia." *Guernica* (blog), November 23, 2020. Accessed November 23, 2020. https://www.guernicamag.com/lost-in-a-misgendered-appalachia/.

Harkins, Anthony. *Hillbilly: A Cultural History of an American Icon*. Oxford: Oxford University Press, 2004.

Harkins, Anthony, and Meredith McCarroll, eds. *Appalachian Reckoning: A Region Responds to* Hillbilly Elegy. First edition. Morgantown: West Virginia University Press, 2019.

Hesford, Wendy S. *Spectacular Rhetorics: Human Rights Visions, Recognitions, Feminisms*. Next Wave. Durham, NC: Duke University Press, 2011.

"Highways and Byways: The People's Rule in Government." *The Chautauquan, A Weekly Newsmagazine*, June (1912). American Periodicals.

Hutton, T. R. C. *Bloody Breathitt: Politics and Violence in the Appalachian South*. Lexington: University of Kentucky Press, 2015.

"Impressions of the Passing Show." *New York Times* (March 24, 1912), section SM16. ProQuest, Historical Newspapers: The New York Times.

Levering, Frank. *Thunder in the Hills*. Directed by Angell Caudill, March 24, 2012.

Lewis, Ronald L. *The Industrialist and the Mountaineer: The Eastham-Thompson Feud and the Struggle for West Virginia's Timber Frontier*. Morgantown: West Virginia University Press, 2017.

Lord, William. *The Red Ear of Corn*. Pittsburg, PA: Tri-Ad Litho, Inc., 1999.

Mann, Etta Donnan. *Four Years in the Governor's Mansion of Virginia*. Richmond, VA: The Dietz Press, 1937.

McGerr, Michael E. *A Fierce Discontent: The Rise and Fall of the Progressive Movement in America, 1870–1920*. Oxford: Oxford University Press, 2005.

Miller, Carolyn R. "Genre as Social Action." *Quarterly Journal of Speech* 70, no. 2 (1984): 151–76.

"Mob Wipe Out Court." *Kansas Baptist Herald* (March 16, 1912) n.p.

Mount Airy Museum of Regional History. "History," n.d. https://www.northcarolinamuseum.org/index.php?option=com_content&view=article&id=56&Itemid=79.

"Mountain Court Is Wiped Out." *Savannah Tribune* (March 23, 1912), 1.

Obermiller, Phillip J., and Shaunna L. Scott. "Making Appalachia: Interdisciplinary Fields and Appalachian Studies." In *Studying Appalachian Studies: Making the Path by Walking*, edited by Chad Berry, Phillip J. Obermiller, and Shaunna L. Scott. Urbana: University of Illinois Press, 2015.

"Obsessions Should Be Shunned." *New York Times* (April 24, 1912), 6.

"Of Course They Are Not Monsters." *New York Times* (March 22, 1912), 8.

"One Caught, Allen Gang Will Give Up." *New York Times* (March 23, 1912), 1.

"Outlaw Once an Officer." *New York Times* (March 17, 1912), 6.

"Outlaws Slay Judge in Court." *New York Times* (March 18, 1912), 1.

"Posses Close In on Allen Outlaws." *New York Times* (March 24, 1912), 13.

Puckett, Anita. "Aftermath of the Courthouse Tragedy." Presented at the Courthouse Tragedy Centennial Symposium, Hillsville, VA, March 13, 2012.

Renwick, Roger DeV. "Ballad." In *American Folklore*. Third edition. edited by Jan Harold Brunvand, 57–61. New York: Garland, 1996.

Ridolfo, Jim, and Danielle Nicole DeVoss. "Composing for Recomposition: Rhetorical Velocity and Delivery." *Kairos* 13, no. 2 (January 15, 2009).

Schneider, Rebecca. *Performing Remains: Art and War in Times of Theatrical Reenactment*. Abingdon, Oxon; New York: Routledge, 2011.

Shapiro, Henry D. *Appalachia on Our Mind: The Southern Mountains and Mountaineers in the American Consciousness, 1870–1920*. Chapel Hill: University of North Carolina Press, 1978.

Sheard, Cynthia Miecznkowski. "The Public Value of Epideictic Rhetoric." *College English* 58, no. 7 (November 1996): 765–794.

"Shoot the Judge." *Wall Street Journal* (March 18, 1912).

"Should Be a Hunt, Not a War." *New York Times* (March 19, 1912), section Voices of the Times. ProQuest, Historical Newspapers: The New York Times.

Smith, John. "Trauma." In *Keywords for Southern Studies*, edited by Scott Romine and Jennifer Rae Greeson, 354–65. Athens: University of Georgia Press, 2016.

Taylor, Diana. *The Archive and the Repertoire: Performing Cultural Memory in the Americas*. Durham: Duke University Press, 2003.

"The Recall at Hillsville." *New York Times* (March 15, 1912).

"Three Killed in Virginia Court: Allen's Gang Illustrates the Recall by Murdering the Judge, Sheriff and Prosecutor." *Wall Street Journal* (March 15, 1912), 6.

Toelken, Barre. "Ballads and Folksongs." In *Folk Groups and Folklore Genres: An Introduction*, edited by Elliot Oring, 147–74. Logan: Utah State University Press, 1986.

"Trap Is Laid for Virginia Outlaws." *New York Times* (March 22, 1912), 3.

Tribe, Ivan. *An Appalachian Family and the Music That Shaped Their Lives.* Urbana-Champagne: University of Illinois Press, 1993.

Bibliography

Tucker, Chad. "Boiling Point." Produced by FOX8 WGHP-TV. *57 Shots in 90 Seconds*, August 17, 2020 Podcast, MP3 Audio, 19. https://art19.com/shows/57-shots-in-90-seconds.

"Two More Dead in Allen Feud." *New York Times* (March 16, 1912) 1.

Waller, Altina L. *Feud: Hatfields, McCoys, and Social Change in Appalachia, 1860–1900*. Chapel Hill: University of North Carolina Press, 1988.

Webb, Bill. Interview with the author, July 8, 2016.

Williams, John Alexander. *Appalachia: A History*. Chapel Hill: University of North Carolina Press, 2002.

Index

Index

Index